PRAISE FOR *A WITCH'S GUIDE TO CRAFTING YOUR PRACTICE*

"The book I wish I'd had when I was first exploring Paganism over a quarter century ago. Not just because it's an excellent foundational text, but also because Lisa McSherry explains so much of the why and how of what is often taken for granted in elementary Craft. And she does a wonderful job of breaking it out of the gender binary and other assumptions that 21st century practice has traded in for more inclusive ways of being and practicing."

—Lupa, creator of the *Tarot of Bones*

"McSherry makes some of the most complex aspects of American eclectic Wicca practice accessible and understandable, all while providing a much-needed update on aspects of the practice. She unchains energy polarity from the limited concept of gender, explains what a Book of Shadows actually does for a practitioner and for theists, shows how deity relationships function in a cooperative manner. This book is a wonderful, inclusive, and academically anchored approach to Wicca that allows beginners to engage with clarity."

—Diana Rajchel, author of *Hex Twisting*

"If you're one of the many people who feel drawn to Wicca and related modern Pagan practices but don't feel comfortable joining a formal tradition, you're in for a treat. Lisa McSherry's *A Witch's Guide to Crafting Your Practice* is the resource you've been waiting for. McSherry walks the reader through the steps necessary to build a personal spiritual practice, from altars and tools to deities, energy work, and ethics. This is not a "quickie" setup but a deep dive into solitary Craft…At the end, you'll have a solid basis for lifelong spiritual practice, and it will have been time well spent."

—Laura Perry, founder and Temple Mom of
Modern Minoan Paganism and third-degree Wiccan priestess

T0035345

A
WITCH'S GUIDE
TO CRAFTING
YOUR
PRACTICE

© L. McSherry

ABOUT THE AUTHOR

Lisa McSherry is an author, Priestess, and world traveler. She leads Jaguar-Moon Coven, which has been teaching the basics of witchcraft since 2000. She is the author of *Magickal Connections: Creating a Healthy and Lasting Spiritual Group* and *The Virtual Pagan 2.0*. She founded the website *Facing North: A Community Resource*, which offers monthly reviews of items of interest to the alternative spirituality community. Visit her online at lisamcsherry.com.

A WITCH'S GUIDE TO CRAFTING YOUR PRACTICE

Create a Magical Path that Works for You

LISA McSHERRY

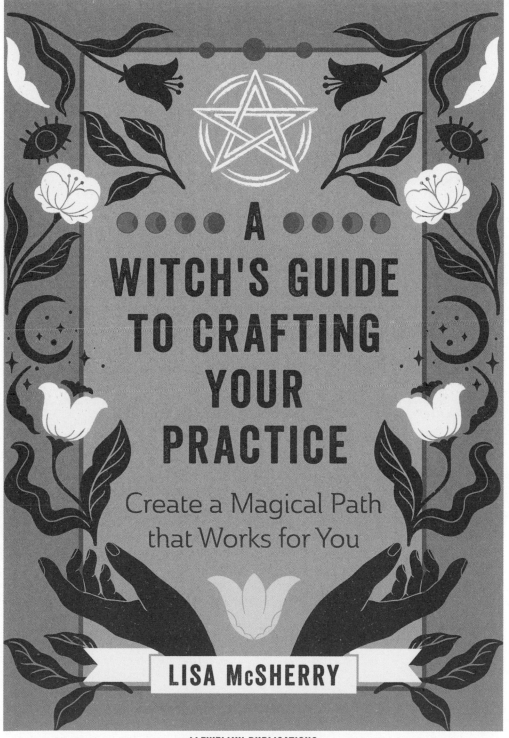

LLEWELLYN PUBLICATIONS
WOODBURY, MINNESOTA

A Witch's Guide to Crafting Your Practice: Create a Magical Path That Works for You © 2022 by Lisa McSherry. All rights reserved. No part of this book may be used or reproduced in any manner whatsoever, including internet usage, without written permission from Llewellyn Publications, except in the case of brief quotations embodied in critical articles and reviews.

FIRST EDITION
First Printing, 2022

Cover design by Shannon McKuhen
Interior art by the Llewellyn Art Department

Llewellyn Publications is a registered trademark of Llewellyn Worldwide Ltd.

Library of Congress Cataloging-in-Publication Data (Pending)
ISBN: 978-0-7387-6980-6

Llewellyn Worldwide Ltd. does not participate in, endorse, or have any authority or responsibility concerning private business transactions between our authors and the public.

All mail addressed to the author is forwarded but the publisher cannot, unless specifically instructed by the author, give out an address or phone number.

Any internet references contained in this work are current at publication time, but the publisher cannot guarantee that a specific location will continue to be maintained. Please refer to the publisher's website for links to authors' websites and other sources.

Llewellyn Publications
A Division of Llewellyn Worldwide Ltd.
2143 Wooddale Drive
Woodbury, MN 55125-2989
www.llewellyn.com

Printed in the United States of America

OTHER BOOKS BY LISA MCSHERRY

Magickal Connections: Creating a Healthy and Lasting Spiritual Group (New Page, 2007)

The Virtual Pagan 2.0 (Independently published, 2021)

The Virtual Pagan (Weiser Books, 2001)

DEDICATION

Para John, sempre.
Casar contigo foi a melhor ideia que tive toda a minha vida.
Vamos continuar a rir, querida.

CONTENTS

ACKNOWLEDGMENTS

Desmond Tutu speaks about his country's idea of *ubuntu*, the fact that we can't exist as humans in isolation; we are interconnected, and what we do affects the whole world. This is particularly true for authors, this book more than most. Decades ago, two people in completely different areas of my life—LM and JK—gave me more responsibility than I thought I could handle; their absolute confidence in me created the seed that became the book you hold in your hands.

All the many students who completed the Art of Ritual class—and perhaps especially those who didn't—taught me so much. Failure teaches as much as success; you helped make the class better with every course correction made over the years.

My teachers come from many places, and all have a piece of this book to their credit. Some have been more direct than others. Most especially Starhawk, who first opened the door.

Since the turn of the century, John Casker has been my partner, helping me keep perspective and balance while sharing his deep wisdom and encouragement. He broadens my horizons and creates wonderful adventures and experiences.

Finally, everyone in JaguarMoon coven past and present, has been my solid support, offering wise counsel, and a willingness to try new things. Together we have created something so much more than any one of us could have seen. I look forward to the coming decades with you as much as I appreciate the ones we've spent together.

INTRODUCTION

"Words are pale shadows of forgotten names. As names have power, words have power. Words can light fires in the minds of men. Words can wring tears from the hardest hearts."[1]

You hold in your hands my distillation of more than four decades of knowledge and experience. I remember how it felt when I was just beginning to find a new spirituality, one that wasn't the faith of my family, one that didn't tell me how sinful I was, just by being born. I didn't know exactly what I was looking for, but I was desperate to find it. When I found the spirituality I practice now, it was almost an accident, and when I tried to find out more, I was so bewildered just trying to find good reliable information.

I am a Witch. I'm also a priestess and founder of a tradition. My perspective is rooted within my understanding of Deity, religion, community, symbols, and the practices embodied within those terms; all of which provide context for how I learn and in turn how I teach. It is not my intention to give you

---

1. Patrick Rothfuss, *The Name of the Wind* (New York: DAW Books, 2007), 617.

the keys to the "One True Way"—quite the opposite. I am the guide along the path you take, helping you avoid thorny brambles and pointing out what looks like the best course. In the end, you must provide your own context and structure for the practices I discuss. Don't worry about doing everything exactly as it is in this book—it is a guidebook, not a rule book. You are the center of your universe and your feet are planted in a specific place unique in space and time that will shape your experience.

If you were wondering, you don't need to be born into a Witch family or receive an initiation to be a Witch. What you do need to do is pay attention to the lessons the Universe offers through your experiences, take responsibility for your actions, and then take action as your ethics and moral compass direct. Witchcraft isn't just for women—it's for men, trans folx, and those with no gender. It's for people who love sex, those who don't have sex, and those who create their own pleasurable experiences. It's for those who feel a call to worship Deity, those who want to become as much a part of the natural cycles of the world as possible, and for those who see working magic as a process devoid of nature or Deity. Witchcraft is an active healing and an act of resistance. Declaring oneself a Witch and practicing magic have everything to do with claiming personal authority and power.

My own perspective is that being a Witch is primarily about understanding that we are divine as any external Deity. What we practice is called an immanent religion, one in which Deity is found within and throughout the universe. To my mind, it is the most empowering and significant modes of faith. Over the course of this exploration of your faith, I will share oceans of knowledge with you: it is part of my mission statement to help you learn to see the difference between con artists and true magic. I hope that you will learn to see your own divine reality—your personal value. That said, a belief in Deity is *not* required to gain a great deal from this material.

It is important that you understand that because this is a text aimed primarily at newcomers to Witchcraft, it inevitably makes generalizations. Pagan traditions and practitioners are infinitely diverse, and counterexamples will be easy to find for any general statement I make. This does not negate the accuracy of those statements. My early teachers were themselves trained in Traditional Wicca and, unsurprisingly, that was hugely influential on my practices as a Witch. From them I learned core practices for working magic, creating sacred space, and writing ritual. Eventually, however, I moved on from their teaching, exploring Witchcraft on my own and with others in a variety of formal and informal spaces. Nonetheless, many structures and core practices I offer throughout this book have their roots in a model rooted within the neopagan ritual framework. Not only it is familiar to me, but it is also a solid foundational structure, easily explained to newcomers. As well, the Witchcraft I discuss and describe is rooted in that of European and American lineage, the primary culture of my teachers, family, and students. Paganism, Witchcraft, and the manner in which people perceive Witches is very different in non-European cultures.

All of which goes to say that although I will occasionally make a sweeping statement that may not be 100 percent true all of the time, please take it as a generalization rather than an absolute. I have done my best to offer you good, solid, tested information about each of the practices that follow.

TERMS OF THE CRAFT

The heart of this lesson revolves around how we describe ourselves and not only to others. Why do we care what we call ourselves? Partly it comes about because humans apply labels to the world around them, a process that seems to be a very efficient way of processing information. Take a moment to think about how many labels for yourself you've used in the week. Here's a few I've used in my life recently: nerd, geek, woman, introvert, and omnivore. I bet that as you read each one, you had a particular concept of what each meant—you were building a picture of me. Labels are what we call ourselves in our heads, the boxes we use to define who we are. We do it to others and we do it to ourselves, and what we whisper to ourselves every day has a significant influence on our self-concept and dictates the tenor of our thoughts and actions. Labels aren't just personal; they function as a part of the shared reality we call society. Researchers discovered that we create labels based on a combination of personal traits, the objects we want to label, and the environment. When other people consistently tell us we are something, whether or not we believe it, we are significantly more likely to incorporate that label into our overall identity. Research shows that our conceptions of ourselves are based almost entirely on what others think of us.

The information in this interlude may seem contradictory at times, reflecting what you will find within the broader community. It includes a variety of perspectives so that you can make your own decisions. There is no central authority, no single external place to look for answers. Knowing that words have meaning and that how we use language to present ourselves and to understand others gives us a start to understanding how we can change the world.

Witch

There is an extra complication for Witches, in that the word "Witch" has negative connotations; "Witchcraft" in any language is almost always associated with things that are evil and destructive. Thus you find that Witches over the centuries have always been whatever a particular culture believed to be evil and feared the most; it usually didn't signify any religious practice or what we would recognize as magical practice. These are the Witches of fairy tales, sermons, and some parts of pop culture. But with the publication of Margaret Murray's *Witch Cult in Western Europe* in 1921, the word began to take on a more positive connotation. Then Gerald Gardner used the word "Witchcraft" to describe his newly created Wiccan religion in the 1950s, adding a definition of "Witchcraft" as it describes a religious practice. In the United States, some authors and publishers began using the words "Wicca" and "Wiccan" instead of Witch or Witchcraft, hoping to avoid (or sidestep, to some degree) any adverse reaction on readers' part, thus further confusing the labeling. There is a saying that not all Witches are Wiccan, but we're all Pagan.

Wicca

Created in the 1940s by Gerald Brosseau Gardner, a retired British civil servant and ordained minister, Wicca combines the Witchcraft taught in the New Forest Coven with modern esoteric practices.[2] The terms "Wicca" and "Wiccen" were first used by Charles Cardell, who developed his tradition of Witchcraft distinct from that of Gardner, in a 1958 article in *Light* magazine.

In the 1960s and 1970s, Wicca spread from the UK to other English-speaking countries and became associated with the burgeoning feminist and environmental movements. In the United States, Scott Cunningham published a series of books in the early 1980s, teaching a version of Wicca based on solitary practice. And the US government first officially recognized Wicca as a religion in 1985.

---

2. Ordained in the Christian sect known as the Ancient British Church.

Aside from a belief in magic, there are few beliefs that all Wiccan traditions share. "Witches perceive of themselves as having left the Father's House (Jewish and Christian religion) and returned 'home' to the Self (Goddess religion) with a call to heal western women's (and men's) alienation from community and spirituality and to become benders of human and societal developments!"[3] This flexibility has, as Michael F. Strmiska says, "allowed people with interest in different deities and religious traditions to customize Wicca to suit their specific interests, thus enhancing the religion's appeal to a broad and growing membership."[4]

I see three kinds of Wiccans:

1. People who are part of British Traditional Witchcraft (generally Gardnerians and Alexandrians) using the term their founder coined. Being able to call oneself Gardnerian requires training and initiation from a lineaged Wiccan; one cannot self-initiate into these traditions.

2. People who look to what is often labeled American Eclectic Wicca, which includes Starhawk, Raymond Buckland, and Scott Cunningham. A crucial part of this group is that self-initiation is an accepted practice and solitary practice is as valid as group participation.

3. People who don't want to be called a "Witch," considering "Wiccan" as less freighted with societal reprobation.

The last group is the most puzzling, but then I've been calling myself a Witch for decades and think the label is comfortable. From my perspective, I have seen many arguments and unhappiness about who gets to call oneself Wiccan, and it's not great for our community. The people in the first group are often frustrated by the others' use (appropriation, even) of a term their founder coined. The people in the second group are often ignorant of the term "Wiccan" having been appropriated; they have been told it's the right term and believe it identifies them.

---

3. Jone Salomonsen, *Enchanted Feminism: The Reclaiming Witches of San Francisco* (London: Routledge, 2002), 282.

4. Michael Strimska, *Modern Paganism in World Cultures: Comparative Perspectives* (Santa Barbara, CA: ABC-CLIO, 2005), 38.

Witchcraft

Witchcraft contains many groups and individuals with connections to each other that are, for the most part, looser than what you will find between those who participate in Judeo-Christian religions. Witches have distinct traditions, beliefs, pantheon, etc., generally revere nature, and use the application of focused energy to accomplish a desired result.

Magick versus Magic

Some add a "k" at the end of the word "magic" to distinguish it from entertainment; others don't. Aleister Crowley invented the word "magick" to distance himself from the magic (no "k") practiced by the Order of the Golden Dawn. The Merriam-Webster, Oxford English, and Cambridge English dictionaries have no listing for the word "magick," although "magik" was used in the fifteenth and sixteenth centuries. Some Witches (notably those in the Cabot line) use "Majik." All are correct; there is no need to fight. Instead, recognize the different lineages for each spelling and understand that each is right for its proponents.

Other Common Terms

What follows is a lexicon of sorts that could serve as a foundation for how you view the materials presented throughout this book and within the alternative spirituality community.

> *Blessed Be:* A phrase uttered within ritual to seal or provide support for a magical act, used in greeting, parting, and general well-wishing. "Blessed be" is an acknowledgment of the deity within and of all present. It confers one's blessing upon another.

> *Pagan:* An umbrella term for anyone not practicing a mainstream religion, such as Buddhism, Christianity, Hinduism, Islam, or Judaism. All Witches are Pagan, most Pagans are not Witches.

> *Ritual:* An ordered sequence of events or actions repeated in the 'same' manner each time to produce an altered state of consciousness, within which specific magical or religious results are obtained. (I can't help but point out that one need not believe in

anything to belong to a religion, although most religious organizations require that one has conforming beliefs to be a member of that religion.)

So Mote It Be: A phrase uttered within ritual to seal or provide support for a magical act, its origin can be traced to Freemasonry, whose prayers have ended with this phrase since 1390.[5] "So Mote it Be" is best thought of as a shortening of the phrase "As I will, so mote it be!" and is the moment when we access our will and issue the command that activates our magical directive.

A longer list of commonly used terms is available in the glossary.

WHY BE A WITCH?

Being a Witch is, in part, about taking control of your life, changing your life to manifest your desires, and healing yourself. It's about getting rid of what doesn't serve you, becoming more you, and aligning with your better self. We create our own magical practice using techniques based on ancient ways. And in my opinion, we do all of that not only to improve ourselves but to change the world for the better.

By blending our own practice with the practices of those we encounter in life, we create powerful magic. My personal practice was developed over four decades in a variety of groups, on my own, with my coven, and the class we've taught since 2000. It's a blend of everything I have learned, experienced, and done. My practice will not and should not be the same as your practice. However, too often this logic gets overextended into the notion that "anything goes." Anything *can* go, but if you don't know the whys and the hows, you're only going nowhere. Creating a unique practice based on a solid core is vital.

This book is meant to be a foundation text or perhaps a gap-filler for everything you've taught yourself so far. In the twenty-plus years I've been teaching, my students have come from all over the globe, from every cultural background and all across the socio-economic landscape. They have given me so much

---

5. Scottish Rite, "Why do Freemasons end their prayers with the phrase 'So mote it be'?" Accessed April 17, 2020. https://scottishrite.org/scottish-rite-myths-and-facts/qa-so-mote-it-be.

knowledge from their own perspectives, broadening my view of the world, and the magic therein.

One of the few absolutes I hold to is that magic is strongest when it comes from the personal symbol library within your soul, and only you can develop that language.

CHOOSING A CRAFT NAME

What's in a name? that which we call a rose.
By any other name would smell as sweet.[6]

While it isn't in any way required, the choosing of a name for use in Craft circumstances (class, rituals, etc.) can be a transformative process. In a sense, taking on a new name represents a shift, a move from your mundane self into someone new—a Witch. While many new Witches choose a Craft name when they first start, it can also be a marker of a deliberate choice to become a Witch. There are many reasons why people in the Craft choose a new name: to represent a change in viewpoint, to mark a new phase in one's growth or maturity, to indicate a personality trait, even to preserve anonymity.

Names are important: they're part of every culture and of enormous importance both to the people who receive them and to those that bestow them. A name identifies you: it's your public face (even when "public" means only a few people). In so many fairy tales, to know someone's (true) name was to have power over them—just look to the German fairytale of *Rumpelstiltskin*. The Egyptian sun god Ra's true name was tricked out of him, allowing Isis to elevate her son, Horus, to the throne. When first captured by Polyphemus, Homer's Odysseus is careful not to reveal his name; when asked for it, Odysseus tells the giant that he is "nobody." But later, having blinded Polyphemus and escaping, Odysseus boastfully reveals his real name. Polyphemus was then able to call upon his father, the sea god Poseidon for revenge. After that, Odysseus faced the relentless hostility of Poseidon, all because he gave up his name.

Many Witches relinquish our given names, symbolically giving up the old and no longer valid; we then take a new name as a symbol of our new life. The taking of a new name calls for deep thought and planning, and a touch of merriment. Most of us choose a name that reflects our personality or our

---

6. William Shakespeare, *Romeo and Juliet*, Act II, scene 2.

interests. Some select the name of a deity that expresses a quality to which they aspire. (A word of caution: when taking on the name of a deity, be careful to research *all* aspects of that deity's persona, as you will be consciously evoking those qualities within yourself. At the same time, you might want to avoid the very highest names in any particular pantheon (i.e., Isis, or Zeus, as it may imply arrogance.) Some take their names from history or mythology, especially those names associated with their particular path in the Craft (Welsh names for Welsh traditions, Irish names for Irish traditions, etc.) Others make up their names entirely.

Some of us are happy with our given name and see no reason to change it. Many of us end up taking more than one Craft name, finding ourselves growing into a name that expresses our true self. Many of us also have a secret Craft name only revealed under specific circumstances. You may also be entirely happy with your birth name and feel no need to change. In which case, there is no need to do so.

More than anything, taking a new name indicates to the larger world that an internal shift has occurred. You are no longer John, or Sally, or Lisa. Instead, you are Rowan Heartwood, PurpleMist Prancer, or Maat. This "new" person has different qualities—a new focus or way of seeing things. She has a different attitude and persona.

A Note about Titles

Some traditions of Witchcraft use the prefixes "Lord" and "Lady" to indicate their coven leaders. Those titles are not part of a public name but are closer to how "Reverend" is used in other religious groups. Using "Lady" or "Lord" in your own craft name is gauche, even a little rude, something only an un- or ill-informed person chooses to do.

Names and Numerology

Whether choosing a new name or keeping your given name, it's interesting to apply basic numerology and see what your name reveals. Is your name, in fact, right for you? To see if it is, look to see if your name number and your birth number are the same. Why should your birth number match your name number? Your birth number is unchanging; we can (and do!) change our name, our address, our online identification, etc., but we cannot change our date of birth.

When we choose a name number that matches our birth number, we align the two vibrations, creating a deep synergy and connection. There are several different numerology systems widely used today. The method below is the one I first learned and still use in working with names.

Find the name number for the name you have chosen by linking all the letters of the alphabet with all the numbers, except zero, see below.

Letter Values in Numerology

As an example, suppose you have chosen the name Diana and your birth date is June 23, 1956. Using the following chart: d=4, i=9, a=1, n=5, a=1. Or, 4+9+1+5+1 = 20, 2+0 = 2. Your birth number would be: 6+2+3+1+9+5+6 =32, 3+2=5.

1	2	3	4	5	6	7	8	9
A	B	C	D	E	F	G	H	I
J	K	L	M	N	O	P	Q	R
S	T	U	V	W	X	Y	Z	

But the numbers for your name and birthdate don't match! One way to fix this would be to add a U or L to the name, changing the spelling to Dianau or Dianal. Doing so makes the name number the same as the birth number of 5. Alternatively, you could choose an entirely different name. Then again, if the qualities of the number of the new name are those you desire to invoke in you consciously, a new name is a perfect choice.

A Quick Meditation to Find a New Name

Inspired by a meditation created by Phoenix McFarland, this meditation can help you discover your craft name.[7]

When you have time, create sacred space.[8] (Make sure your phone is turned off, that no one will bother you, and that you have silenced any alarms.) Your sacred space can be as formal as you desire.

Invoke Deity using your own words, asking it to grant you deeper self-knowledge. Ask for a name and wait for an answer. If none is immedi-

---

7. *The New Book of Magical Names* (St. Paul, MN: Llewellyn Publications, 2003), 46.

8. If you've forgotten how or jumped ahead, see chapter 9 for a refresher.

ately forthcoming, make a list of your best qualities (for example, smart, funny, strong, creative, witty, etc.), then, make a list of things you like. (My list includes music, water, moon, crystal, and cats.) Look at the two lists you created and see if a name jumps out at you or pops into your head. If not, you may want to add a third list of qualities you want to invoke within yourself. (This might best be done in a second ritual if you still can't think of a new name.) Sit with the lists for a bit and contemplate what a new you might look like to others.

If you don't get an answer, stop before you get frustrated. Ask Deity to reveal your name to you and thank It for the help already given. Close the sacred space and place the lists on your altar.

Over the next few days, think about the lists you wrote. Pay attention to your dreams and meditations. The name will come to you.

Although it may take a while to find a name you like that is also numerologically correct, it's worth it. Choosing your new name should be given considerable thought and time, as well as an unrushed process.

My Naming Story

For the years I practiced solitary, I remained simply Lisa. (What can I say? I like my name.) I researched my name and discovered that if I chose to believe that Lisa came from Melissa (rather than Elizabeth), I could even have a cool origin story. Elizabeth means "chosen of God" or some such thing, but the Melissae were priestesses of either Demeter or Aphrodite in ancient Greece. Very cool.

Then I joined a formal coven and felt that I needed to choose a new name. There were many things changing in my life at that time, not just joining the coven, and I decided to use LisaDawn. The "Lisa" is an homage to my "mundane" name, and the "Dawn" a symbol of my new life's beginning. As I progressed through the coven, I kept that name until my Second Degree initiation. At that time, I chose the name Maat, in honor of the Egyptian Goddess of Law, Ma'at (note the slight, but crucial difference) She who *is* Order, Keeper of Justice, Merciful One. I felt that I wanted to evoke her qualities of merciful justice and maintainer of order within me.[9] My last name change came when I received my Third degree and hived off to form JaguarMoon. This name is what I would call my private name, and I do not use it except for particular, formal, JaguarMoon-specific rituals. This private name corresponds to the number nine, and I chose it to invoke all of that number's qualities within myself as a leader and teacher.

---

9. Taking the name of a deity should not be done lightly, because you are embodying its aspects within yourself ... all of them. To become Coyote, for example, because you admire its strength and cleverness is fine *if* you realize that he is the Great Trickster who will view your admiration as a fine joke and turn your life topsy-turvy at every opportunity.

FOUNDATION

Welcome to your first lessons.
We start with the
foundations of our Craft:
tracking our journey as Witches
and creating an altar.
These are practical lessons,
a gentle easing into
the life of a Witch.

PART 1

Chapter 1
BOOK OF SHADOWS

We humans have this habit of justification when it comes to magic, astrology, psychic readings—all of the psychic abilities! It's so easy to ignore all the times when the information was wrong, or the spell didn't work or whatever. Our attention wants to focus on the times that it DOES appear to work, especially with hindsight. This is one of the benefits of a magical notebook. It keeps us from fooling ourselves, from placing our faith in false dreams and hopes. It keeps us from walking off cliffs before we are ready to be the Fool.[10]

Philosopher George Santayana once said, "Those who cannot remember the past are condemned to repeat it," something that is especially true for those of us standing at the crossroads and moving beyond the mainstream. Thus, one of the essential tools of a Witch is the Book of Shadows or the Witch's notebook, self-created and self-maintained. Your book isn't just a collection of gathered knowledge but a chronicle of the journey from beginner to wherever you'd like it to end. Keeping accurate records of your magical workings is necessary for any Witch, but especially so for a solitary who doesn't have the support of a

---

10. From my Book of Shadows, circa 1998.

15

larger group for feedback, direction, or guidance. Your book is where you track your progress—and your failures! Failures teach us far more than our successes, giving us insight into areas we will want to develop and explore. Failures offer an early-warning system for psychic or psychological issues we'll want to delve into to become better people. The book will come to be its own kind of early warning system, that reveals patterns previously obscured by the seeming randomness of daily life. If you still need more reason to write it all down, consider the research that keeping notes while reading improves your memory and recall of the information.

Witchcraft is a belief system of growth founded on the expectation of personal and spiritual growth. Naturally, as we grow and change, our book evolves to fit our new needs and perspectives. I started with an oversized black-covered sketchbook/journal in which I wrote my first desires as a Witch, my explorations, snatches of reading, and the daily encounters that revealed a magical world. Not long after, I also started a dream journal, a tarot journal, and a regular journal. When I began taking formal classes in the late 1990s and found my way online, I started keeping the information given to me in a bunch of three-ring binders. Years later, a scanner let me store this information on my computer, organized into folders for easy reference. My nearly forty-year journey deeper into Witchcraft has changed me, and my book has evolved right alongside. I can reach out and pick up one of my first dream journals and be instantly reminded of the dream of the man from Mars, and what happened in my physical life that made that dream valuable. And why that dream is important to me, even today. (Because I wouldn't have opened my journal to that particular dream if it wasn't valuable to me now.)

The keeping of a Book of Shadows is a lifetime endeavor, time to start one now.

A BIT OF HISTORY

As glamorous as the idea of the term "Book of Shadows" being ancient is, evidence shows that it comes from the founder of Wicca, Gerald Gardner, in the early to mid-twentieth century. The *Gardnerian Book of Shadows* is the most well-known, being the root source of the ritual material of the various traditions that make up the strain of Witchcraft known as British Traditional Wicca (BTW), the source of many practices in modern Witchcraft. Gardner claimed that the practice of keeping such a book was ancient, and the reason there were none older than his was because they had been burned after a Witch died. I admit it's a romantic notion but a bit ridiculous when you consider Witchcraft's roots in the European countryside. Most people couldn't read or write until reasonably modern times, and the cost of paper and bookbinding would have been prohibitive for almost everyone, especially those outside cities.[11]

Moreover, while Gardner claimed the term "Book of Shadows," his High Priestess, Doreen Valiente, notes that he read the phrase in the magazine *The Occult Observer*, maintaining that "It was a good name, and it is a good name still, wherever Gardner found it."[12] Janet Farrar and Gavin Bone have proposed that Gardner took the name from Sufism:

> The Book of Shadows in Sufi practice is a method of divination, involving taking a measure of head, chest, and height. The measurements are then compared to notes within the book. As noted by Ron Hutton in *The Triumph of the Moon*, there was a Sufi among Gardner's circle: Idries Shah, author of *The Way of the Sufi*.[13]

All of which tells modern seekers that if the author of a Book of Shadows (by any name) claims the book is centuries-old or has Valiente's poetry in it, we have to question the claim of the book's age.[14]

MODERN USAGE

In many traditions and among many solitary practitioners, the Book of Shadows is entirely independent of Gardner's original. With the advent of the internet, it is relatively easy to find whole books online, even Gardner's supposedly oath-bound book. However, most of these postings are collections of data, spells, and (occasionally) articles. These collections can be source material for your workings, but I wouldn't try to copy from them wholesale—you'll have plenty to add to your Book as you grow and develop your practice.

---

11. George Santayana, *The Life of Reason, Vol. I, Reason in Common Sense*, 1905.

12. Doreen Valiente, *The Rebirth of Witchcraft* (London: Robert Hale, 1989), 51.

13. Janet Farrar and Gavin Bone, *Progressive Witchcraft: Spirituality, Mysteries, and Training in Modern Wicca* (Boston: Red Wheel/Weiser, 2003), 17.

14. An infamous example is *Lady Sheba's Book of Shadows* published in the 1980s.

In JaguarMoon, new initiates are given a copy of the coven's Book of Shadows at their First Degree Initiation. The coven book consists of information about our tradition, how we came to be, our laws, structure, evolution requirements, and a collection of esoteric information specific to our practices. Although sharing the book with non-coven members is not allowed, nothing in the book is exceptionally secret. We each keep our own books of shadows, which we started in the early days of the Art of Ritual class if we didn't have one before taking the class.

PRIVACY, SECRECY, AND ATTRIBUTION

One decision you will need to make at the outset is whether anyone else will see your book. Will you show any part of it to a coven sib, for example, or a lover? It might be the wisest course to take a few precautions to maintain confidentiality all through the life of your book. At the least, I suggest that when you mention another person, always use their Craft name or just initials (classic, but not a good idea if you later can't remember whether you were referring to Michael Corleone or Marie Curie). That way, if another person sees your book, you won't be inadvertently revealing them as Witches. If you copy someone else's work (ritual, poetry, etc.), always note the author and where you found it. Consider locking your book away if you share your living space with another; it's one of the few tools I would say is so personal you never want another to handle it without your permission. Finally, consider how you want your book handled when you die. I know that may seem like a long way away, but it is inevitable. Do you want it handed to a trusted person for safekeeping and archiving? Burned, buried, or buried at sea? (If so, who will do that for you?)

NO JUDGMENT!

The most important thing to remember about creating a Book of Shadows is that it is a personal and intimate reflection of you—this book will become an integral part of your path. Don't let your inner critic keep you from creating and maintaining your book.

GETTING STARTED

Start by doing. I know, it's easy to say, yet feels so hard to do. Prime the pump by asking yourself a couple of questions about what suits you.

+ What is your style? Neat and organized, creatively cluttered, or somewhere in between?

+ What makes you happy to use? Beautiful, functional, or somewhere in between?

+ How do you keep information? Are you a bit of a packrat, a winnower, or somewhere in between?

+ How much time do you have to spend updating your book? Barely any, as much as you need, or somewhere in between?

Someone who needs their book organized and neat might consider a binder with A to Z tab inserts, information entries printed out, and a section of lined paper to write out their thoughts. A creatively cluttered Witch who needs it to be beautiful might prefer a handmade book with a cover decorated with images that speak deeply to their inner selves and written in with different colored inks.

No matter your personality or style, I urge you to include an index to track entries. And handwriting (rather than typing) is an excellent way to make the important stuff stick in your head. For example, when I need to do a spell, I research it in my reference books and then handwrite it out for my needs (I never use what others have created verbatim; my symbol library is always different). Afterward, I type out the whole activity in my journal, including how it turns out (a valuable part of the learning process).

If you think you have horrid handwriting, type everything and consider unusual fonts to personalize the material. Above all, remember to keep it readable! There are some gorgeous fonts out there that are unreadable for all the text on a page. Or when trying to read it by candlelight. I have to warn you about the calligraphy trap. Calligraphy looks lovely and makes impressive documents; however, it is nearly impossible to read in anything but steady light.

Similarly, be careful of using light-colored inks. One of my students was a calligrapher by trade, and he chose to use a silver ink pen to write down everything. After his first ritual, he gave up and started a new book, having been unable to read anything by flickering candlelight.

Having a journal that combines my dreams, daily life, and magical explorations is what works best for me. It is handwritten and slightly disorganized, but I'm finding I don't need to use this book as a reference as much as it is a map of my journey. Reading the seemingly random juxtapositions often provides insight that my linear-bound computer cannot.

You can always copy by hand what you've collected on your computer (or in your binders).

Don't let a supposed lack of artistic ability keep you from adding artwork. No judgment, remember? Art makes the impact and emotional content of each page stand out. The use of stamps, inks, coloring pens, tracings, and glued images makes the book of someone like me, who cannot draw worth a darn, beautiful.

Keep in mind that it's not just how your book looks, although we are primarily visual beings. How your book feels in your hands, its weight, and heft must be pleasing and exciting to you. How it smells is just as important. While I'm not sure how it would work with a physical book, your electronic version can certainly include recordings of rituals, music, spoken word, anything that feels appropriate.

It may seem like a small thing, but you want your work to hold up for years without the pages turning yellow, cracking, or disintegrating. Avoid this damage by always looking for the words "acid-free" or "archival" on any element you incorporate into your book. (Yes, this means that homemade is not archival without a lot of effort.)

ORGANIZING SUGGESTIONS

A few steps will help increase your organization, and therefore, the value of your gathered knowledge.

1. Index your data. The first or last pages of every binder or book can be devoted to an index of where to look for critical elements. Be detailed because it will make your life easier. If you keep your data on your computer, you might separate it into subfolders (e.g., Animal, Astrology, Aura, etc.). You might also use sub-subfolders in some categories, such as Healing, Home, Love, et cetera, under Spells.

2. Treat your data seriously and make time to organize it on an ongoing basis, even as you gather it. There is nothing worse than facing a pile of data and spending a day (or more) doing nothing but sorting it.

3. Make time to purge your data regularly. Maybe once a year as part of a sabbat tradition.[15] If you aren't sure whether you should trash a piece of data, move it to a different place and see if you reference it even once in the next year. If not, toss it—it held no value for you. I know this feels like heresy, but you will come to understand that you don't need everything you've collected in your travels. We don't keep copies of our first-grade spelling books, after all!

Making a Book by Hand

Making your own Book of Shadows is a lot of fun and allows you the most variety and customization, especially if you make paper and ink. You can infuse handmade paper with scent or herbs.

Materials Needed
Scissors
Ruler
Heavy cardstock or lightweight cardboard (for cover and back)
Paper (for inside the journal)
Piece of paper, different colored or weight from the other paper used
Pencil
¼ inch paper punch
1½ yards string or ribbon (for lacing)
Matboard (for cover art)
Acrylic paint (3 to 4 coordinating colors, light to dark, of your choice)
Cosmetic sponge (for applying paint)
Tacky glue

Instructions
1. Cut two pieces of cover material to the desired size for your book ¼ inch larger all around than the paper you will use. (For example, if your inside pages are 5.5 x 8.5 inches, the cover pieces need to be 6 x 9 inches.)

---

15. I recommend a harvest-based sabbat such as Lammas, although the quieter time of Imbolc might work as well.

2. Cut inside journal paper ¼ inch smaller on all sides than the cover. (Typical paper is 8.5 x 11 inches and cutting that in half makes pages that are 8.5 x 5.5 inches, ideal for a book that you can carry around. It also makes for a lot less cutting and waste.)

3. Measure and mark the placement of binding holes ½ inch in from the left edge on a piece of paper. These markings will be your template for punching holes in each piece of paper and front and back cover. An odd number of holes is attractive.

4. Stack papers between covers, aligning punched holes. Double up the ribbon and insert it through the bottom hole of the front book cover and pull through the back book cover, so there is an even amount of ribbon on both sides of the book. (The ribbon end pulled through the front book cover will be referred to as "Ribbon A," and the ribbon end pulled through the back book cover will be referred to as "Ribbon B.") Crisscross the ribbons to make an X along the binding. Insert Ribbon A through the next to bottom hole on the back book cover and pull through the front book cover. Then, insert Ribbon B through the next to bottom hole on the front book cover and pull through the back book cover. Crisscross the ribbons again along the binding and continue weaving until you have reached the top of the punched holes.

   Tie both ribbon ends into a bow along the side of the binding. Or, you can thread Ribbon B through the top hole on the front book cover so that both Ribbon A and Ribbon B are on the front of the book. Tie the ribbon ends into a bow, cut off any excess, and neaten.

5. To decorate the cover, cut the matboard to the desired size. Lightly sponge paint over the board's surface, using darker color first, then lighter. Let dry.

6. Glue cut-outs onto the painted mat board. Glue matboard onto the front of the cover.

You can decorate your cover much more elaborately than just sponge painting. Stamps and various colored inks are easy to use, as are color prints of symbols you find attractive or compelling. You might also want to glue objects onto the board to add a three-dimensional component.

Creating Magical Ink

We have used inks since the time of the Egyptian pharaohs, nearly 4,500 years ago. Carbon, red ocher, and green malachite were finely ground and made into small cakes. Adding gum and water to these cakes created a liquid that would flow smoothly through the pen (typically a quill, reed, or brush) and then adhere to the writing surface when dry. In the Middle Ages, soot added to gum Arabic or glue made ink, often with a drop of honey added to keep it from becoming brittle. The resulting mixture was a thick black ink that had an almost oily look to it.[16] And for the record: "dragon's blood" and "dove's blood," both commonly sold as magical inks, are not actual blood but instead herbal compounds.

Black Ink
Materials needed
½ t lamp black
1 egg yolk
1 t gum arabic
½ C honey

Instructions
Mix the egg yolk, gum arabic, and honey together. Stir in the lamp black to produce a thick paste that you can store in a sealed container. To use the ink, mix this paste with a small amount of water to achieve the desired consistency.

Brown Ink
Materials needed
4 t loose tea or 4 to 5 black tea bags
1 t gum arabic
½ C boiling water

---

16. NIIR Board of Consultants and Engineers, *Modern Technology of Printing & Writing Inks (with Formulae & Processes) 2nd revised edition,* (Delhi, India: Asia Pacific Business Press, 2016), 299.

Instructions

Pour the boiling water over the tea and steep for about 15 minutes. Squeeze as much liquid as possible from the tea or teabags. Stir in the gum arabic and mix until you have a consistent solution. Strain the ink so that you are left with a thick paste, and allow it to cool completely before bottling.

Consider adding a bit of scent to your ink to intensify the magical properties and effects. Be careful and experiment with this; a small amount of scent goes a long way in changing the ink's consistency.

Here's a quick list of oils and their attributions:

Bergamot: abundance, confidence

Cedar: courage, strength, success

Eucalyptus: healing, protection

Geranium: balance, harmony

Lavender: peace, happiness

Rose: love

Sandalwood: protection, spirituality

WHAT GOES IN YOUR BOOK?

An utterly blank book can be daunting, I know. What to put first in your book? Many people like to start with a blessing, a thoroughly modern (and lovely) convention. If you see writing in your Book of Shadows as a magical act and one that can be imbued with potent energy, beginning the book with a blessing is a good idea, augmenting its energy and intent. When done at the outset, a blessing eliminates stray negative energy carried over from its making (mainly if you purchased the book rather than making your own). The blessing you incorporate will be based primarily on what interests you.

There are some beautiful book blessings available online, and some of my favorites are not even Pagan in orientation. That said, I prefer my own words to others:

My life is yours, Lord and Lady
A journey's map, unfolding, ever-expanding.
I dedicate these words to thee, as I do my life.
So Mote it Be! Blessed Be!

Remember that there will be no judgment about what you put into the book. Moreover, I can almost guarantee that what you start with is not what you will stick with over time. Since our tools are such personal extensions of ourselves, I think it is difficult to tell someone what they "have to" do when building one, and this is especially true for the Book of Shadows—after all, not many of us are going to make our athame or chalice. Most authors will put a long list of items here, a laundry list/checklist, but I am reluctant to do so.

Some things to consider:

+ How portable will your book need to be? Will it accompany you to rituals outside or in other places than your home?
+ Will you be sharing or showing it, to others?
+ How much privacy do you have? Do you live with non-Witches who might snoop? Can you lock your book away (do you need to)? Do you have pets that might chew on the book or sleep on it if left open?
+ Where will you be adding to your book? Will you be at a desk or in a sacred space? Will you want to add to it when in a class?

You are beginning a never-ending journey of spiritual development, one that will only end when you choose. Your Book of Shadows will record the path you travel and provide great insight.

If you insist on direction about what to put in your book, here are some ideas:

+ Your family tree: many Witches work with their ancestors. Putting in a family tree or noting where your family "came from" can be a starting point. I worked with my ancestors on a specific working for a year, which involved offering them food they would enjoy. Knowing that my background is primarily Irish with a healthy dose of central European allowed me to settle on an offering of boiled and mashed potato with honey and paprika. I set out a dish handed down to me

from my Irish grandmother and a candlelit in a holder from my Polish grandmother.[17]

+ Spells, rituals, and all magical workings: I hope this is a bit obvious,
but your Book is a chart of your life as a Witch, and doing magic is
usually a significant part of that life.

+ Your health: Knowing yourself includes paying attention to the physical envelope which carries you through this life. Tracking its ups and
downs can be a valuable aspect of your book. If nothing else, look at
your energy over time—does it vary by season or the amount of sleep
you get? Does the moon's cycle affect you? If you menstruate, noting whether it affects you and how can also be informative. For years,
my moon flow started with the full moon, something I wouldn't have
known if I weren't charting it in my Book of Shadows.

+ Lunar and solar cycles: Some believe that solar flares affect energy,
and many believe that doing magic during the period when the moon
is void of course is a waste of energy. Knowing the moon phase and
zodiac sign it's moving through can be a crucial component of spell
work.

+ Your dreams: Lots of information comes to you through your dreams.
Themes become apparent when you track your dreams, and the information transforms from haphazard or useless to valuable. A Witch of
my acquaintance once told me about a complicated working she'd done
that ultimately failed. We talked it through a bit, and something I said
made her go back to look at her dreams where she found a critical piece
that she needed to know. She redid the working with the new information, and it succeeded perfectly.

+ Divination results: Like tracking your magical workings, it makes
sense to track all the divinations you do. What techniques are you
using? How do you feel afterward? Are some methods more accurate
than others?

---

17. A bundle of letters from ancestors was unearthed by my father during this year. The letters
revealed new branches of the family—perhaps they were feeling left out!

+ Noteworthy events: Conversations with friends, coincidences, *déjà vu*—all of these can be meaningful when seen through the lens of hindsight.

As you create your book, keep your purpose in mind over the days, months, and years that follow. The book is utterly unique and entirely yours in a way rarely found anymore. There are no rules, only some guidelines and previously forged trails to help you get to what you want to manifest. The Book of Shadows is your first tool, completely unique to you. Enjoy its creation and celebrate its evolution!

Activity

+ If you don't have a Book of Shadows, create one. At the least, buy a blank book and start taking notes. Use it while reading to track questions and comments; use it to take notes and make observations.
+ Bless or consecrate your book. Describe what you did.

Bonus Activity: Book of Shadows Attunement

Needed

+ An incense you find pleasing (sandalwood is always good)
+ A small bowl of rice or grain
+ Salt, at least three pinches worth
+ Three drops of essential oil (I recommend sandalwood) mixed with a carrier oil.

Light the incense and walk in a circle around where you will work. Imagine the smoke pushing any negative energy away. Get comfortable and place your Book of Shadows on your lap. Hold your breath for a moment, listening to the stillness, or perhaps your heartbeat. Close your eyes, take three deep breaths, and try to clear your mind. Sit calmly and feel your energies intertwine with the book.

Take up the bowl of rice and blow gently on the grains for a count of three. As you do so, let a little of your personal essence mix with your breath; feel it joining with the energy of the book. Add three pinches of salt to the rice, saying:

> *A pinch of salt clears all harm*
> *Clears the energy, bless this charm*

Dab a bit of the oil on your chest over your heart, at your third eye, and on each palm. Dab it on the book saying:

> *With this oil*
> *We join our journey*
> *Through life's coil*
> *As I will, so mote it be!*

Hold the book in your lap and feel its energies; allow them to join with your own. Feel peaceful and centered and enjoy the comfort. Finish by saying:

> *I am ready to be a Witch*

Chapter 2
CREATE YOUR ALTAR

If your altar is not active, your voice will not be strong.[18]

If you don't already have an altar, it's time to set one up! Creating an altar is fun to do and very fulfilling. It can also seem confusing—there's a ton of controversy out there about what makes a proper altar and what doesn't.

I grew up in a house filled with altars, although my Catholic-raised mother would never use that term. Found in places where it was natural to pause and move from one space to another, they were different kinds of flat surfaces covered with small objects of importance, usually with a theme (although that wasn't always obvious). On the table in the hallway was a collection of sea-tumbled rocks nestled in a woven seagrass basket next to a pretty glass cup and a single birthday candle in a faerie-themed holder. A shelf at the doorway between two rooms featured a glazed pinch pot holding feathers from the songbirds in our garden and a spider web drawing. Everywhere I looked, these small offerings to beauty and to nature were the blueprints for my current altar

---

18. Attributed to Steven Chuks Nwaokeke.

and within my home. My altars are visual clues to stop and take a centering breath even when caught up in the whirlwind of daily life.

When we create a personal altar, we create sacred space and open ourselves to something larger than ourselves. Creating an altar gives us a place to find what connects us to the infinite universe. Altars—places of prayer, ritual, and meditation—simultaneously acknowledge the sacredness inherent in the very space we inhabit and our connection to something greater than ourselves. An altar in and of itself does not make space sacred; it marks what has been there all along. A group of meaningful objects, no matter how precious, does not create an altar. It is the addition of intention that makes the space sacred.

Creating a home altar has ancient roots in many cultures. When I traveled through Italy, I saw how ancient household altars were vital to daily life. Each household had personal deities, often called *lares*, kept safely in a shrine and placed at the table during family meals and banquets. The lares were divine witnesses to all momentous family occasions such as marriages, births, and adoptions. In Japan, household altars are ubiquitous and vary by religion: the Shinto *kamidana*, the Buddhist *butsudan*, and the non-specific *tamadana* (spirit shelf). All act as ritual areas for ancestor veneration. In Mexico, the practice of keeping a home altar traces back to the indigenous Aztec and Toltec peoples. Their altars are a beautiful expression of faith, art, and cultural heritage.

An altar can be as simple or elaborate as your time and resources allow you to manifest. It is impossible to set up a personal altar and not get it right. Deity doesn't care whether the altar is perfect; perfection is in your eye alone. Elaborate altars are made of costly precious woods and adorned with gold, silver, and gems, covered by the finest of fabrics. Altars are also made of scraps of wood and adorned by wildflowers and objects precious only in the owner's eyes. Deity finds both equally beautiful.

Creating and maintaining an altar is highly recommended for the Witch, almost as much as your Book of Shadows. Permanency, however, is not required. For years I lived with others, non-Witches all, and had to be creative about my altar. Sometimes I locked altar items away in a trunk, bringing them out only for ritual work. Other times, my altar occupied a shelf or dresser top behind a cabinet or closet door. One friend travels so much that she only has a portable altar contained entirely within a tin that once held mints. Another has both children and pets in a small apartment—his altar comes out of a box when he is doing ritual, and the stone bowl he uses for a chalice becomes his focus when he meditates.

Altars are always round. Altars are always square. Altars are always spherical. (Yes, now I'm a bit silly.) The point is that other than having a flat surface to place items on, an altar's shape is whatever best meets your needs.

ALTAR PLACEMENT

You may wonder where the best place to create an altar may be, and I think your physical space determines placement. Many of us place our altar in the room or area in the home we spend the most time. Some believe it should be visible from the bed, a haven of thought and quiet; others prefer theirs more centrally located, providing a constant reminder to stop and reflect throughout the day. We build altars in workplaces, bathrooms, and kitchens; no room or placement is inappropriate for sacred space.

Generally, the manner in which you orient your altar is a matter of personal choice rather than a requirement. The simplest way is using the four directions, thereby linking the interior domestic space to the wild world outside.

Different cultures assign different qualities to the four directions, so a bit of research can offer ideas and guidelines to consider for yourself. In the many decades of having an altar, I've placed them all over my home. Below is a very personal collection of what I think about altar placement.

> **Altar in the Center:** This is the best placement for group rituals as everyone can access everything on the altar or place their hands on an object such as a cauldron or cord. It requires a relatively large amount of space to move around easily, and the altar itself needs to be pretty sturdy as it will get bumped, and you don't want it to tip over.

> **Altar in the East:** One of the two most common placements.[19] Many people associate this direction with elemental air, related to the qualities of thought, inspiration, and communication. The sun rises in the east, so the energy here is that of new beginnings. Suitable for new moon workings and any ritual incorporating divination, east is

---

19. Michael P. Foley, *Why Do Catholics Eat Fish on Friday?: The Catholic Origin to Just About Everything* (London: Palgrave Macmillan, 2005), 164.

the direction most often associated with spring and growth, birth, and childhood.

Altar in the North: The other most common placement, as the oft-associated qualities of elemental earth bring steadiness and balance. Suitable for full moon rituals and any workings where you want steady energy. It is the direction of winter and resting, reflection, and self-discovery.

Altar in the West: This direction corresponds with the element of water; its energies relate to emotions, psychism, and the underworld. The direction of the setting sun, an altar in the west is suitable for workings involving death, past lives, and shadow work. It is the direction of autumn and harvest, letting go, and moving on.

Altar in the South: Probably the least common placement, this direction harnesses the qualities of desire and the will. This placement is suitable for workings involving passion, goals, and sexuality. It is the direction of summer and productivity, empowerment, and maximal energy.

Outdoor Altars

If you are lucky enough to have private space outdoors, then consider creating an altar there. Whatever shape or form it takes, build it with intent and pleasure. You might try to set your altar outdoor near trees and plant flowers that will attract birds, butterflies, and bees.

Garden altars: Celebrate nature by becoming a part of the total environment. You may wish to place a flowering plant on it (rather than cut flowers) or place a birdbath nearby. If you place a few stones in the bath, butterflies may sit and sip from the water.

Tree altars: Literally root us into the symbolism of life force, reaching from their roots in the underworld up through to the vastness of the sky. A living tree is usually the core of this altar to which you would add offerings. These offerings might be flowers planted at the base and encircled with stones; some crystals, or even prayers tied to branches. (In Ireland, I saw trees tied with strips of cloth near a "clootie well," a well whose water is known for its healing properties. The strips were a kind of prayer for the health of a specific person. It seemed to me that these trees had become altars.)

Earthwork altars: These are usually dedicated to rituals honoring the solstices; a famous example is Newgrange in Ireland. These altars may be of any shape, although circular and serpentine are common. If you choose to plant herbs or flowers on the earthworks, it can be a charming way to celebrate the seasons.

PORTABLE ALTARS

Creating a portable altar is simplicity itself. Almost two decades ago, a friend of mine left America to begin a series of jobs in the foreign service and asked me to create a portable altar for him. I found a wooden box, about 8" x 8" x 6" with a sliding top. Inside, I put a white votive candle, a small box of stick incense, a vial of sea salt, a small ceramic dish, a feather, a silk scarf, and a few items with special meaning for him. It all fit perfectly and was unobtrusive. He has since told me several times how perfect it is and how grounded he continues to feel, despite being far away from home.

To create a portable altar, choose representations of the four elements: earth, air, water, and fire. Salt or a small pentacle could represent earth; you might also use a tiny pottery dish or a stone. A feather or incense represents air. A candle (and a lighter or book of matches) represents fire. Water is usually available, but a seashell would be an excellent symbol to include. Decide whether you want to place the items in a bag or a box. If space is at a premium, a bag is probably the best idea, especially when it can double as an altar cloth.[20] If you are concerned that your altar items might get damaged, go with a box.

---

20. To make a circular piece of material into a carrying bag, stitch a ½" hem around the edge of the cloth and run a cord through it. Knot the cord at the ends. When you pull the cord tight, it will create a drawstring bag.

A film canister containing a penny, a feather, a match, and a thimble made the tiniest portable altar I have ever seen.[21]

SEASONAL ALTARS

It's lovely to rearrange your altar based on qualities of the season, refreshing it every equinox (spring/fall) and solstice (summer/winter).

A spring altar could have a light green, yellow, or pale blue cloth. A bunch of flowers, flowering branches, or newly sprouting bulbs would be meaningful. All green stones are appropriate, as are pink and pale blue colored stones. Creatures specific to the season would include birds and frogs. You might place the altar in the east.

An autumn altar would look lovely with a cloth of red, orange, or bright blue. Dried flowers or wheat offer up thanks for the season, and all red or orange stones are appropriate. You might consider offering seasonal fruits such as berries or apples, but remember to change them out often. Squirrels and bears are excellent animal symbols for this season. You might place the altar in the west.

A summer altar might have a cloth of bright yellow or deep blue. Any flowers blooming at this time would be appropriate, but especially roses or jasmine with their heady scent. All yellow and blue stones are lovely symbols for the sun, sky, and water. All big cats symbolize summer but lions more than others, and I think crabs and other shellfish have wisdom to offer at this time. You might place the altar in the south.

A winter altar could feature a cloth of white, red, dark green, or even black. Using pinecones, sprigs of holly, or any evergreen foliage is appropriate. All clear and white stones are appropriate. Geese and owls are symbols for this season, as are wolves. You might place this altar in the north.

Altar Descriptions

Deciding what to use for your altar setup, placing it, and then placing objects on it can be very powerful. Creating an altar is the first step in creating sacred space, and there is no single way to do so. What is right for you may not be for another, and what you start with is almost definitely not what you will stay

---

21. Described in my Book of Shadows.

with over time. If you still don't know where to begin, here are descriptions of some of my students' altars:

Aislinn: My altar is my grandmother's cedar chest made by my Scottish grandfather. On it are a copper cauldron, a woven willow basket holding the names of those in my prayers, goddess and god figures, a censer, chalice, sterling silver salt holder with a top, and a crystal bowl for water. There is always something seasonal on my altar; right now, it's the last of the wild roses. When I first set it up, I didn't know about "magnetic north" so I'm truly not sure which direction it faces!

Autumn Embers: My altar lives a dual existence: during the day it looks like any other small chest; at night it becomes a magical platform. I don't feel comfortable with altar being set up since I am living in my parents' home and they do not feel comfortable with my practices. Sometimes I am able to set up an altar in the back yard underneath the broad branches of a maple tree. I prefer this altar since I "feel" more in tune with the energies. Other days my altar is a fairly smooth patch of beach sand not far from my home.

BlueMoonGazer: I use a hutch in my family room where I spend a lot of time; I wanted it where I could see it daily. It sits on a north wall and is white with wooden knobs and tops. I have a 2-gallon fish tank sitting in the middle of it with a red betta fish; on either side are two candles, one gold and one silver that sit in glass candle holders to represent the Lady and the Lord, my incense burner, and two shallow glass bowls with a leaf design for the water and salt.

Creating an altar begins manifesting your feelings and thoughts about the sacred physically, bringing them into full consciousness. When we talk about our altars, some refer to the process of seeking the self: energy, direction, meaning. Others address the state of mind: peacefulness, calm, strength. Usually we talk about connecting to or finding the sacred in daily life, focusing on something "more" than the self and daily prayer, meditation, and communication.

Creating an altar is not simply decorating a room; it is a search for meaning or a process of discovering what has personal meaning. The altar symbolizes the sacred space of the larger circle, an act of magic in and of itself. You will place tools and objects on the altar to represent all the energies of the circle you will be creating throughout your studies in this class.

Activity

Create an altar: If you have had your altar for a while, I suggest you give it a good cleaning and rededicate it to the work of Deity.

Dedicate your altar as sacred: Describe your altar in your Book of Shadows.

Journal: In your Book of Shadows, write the answers to these questions:

+ What is an altar? Is it necessary?
+ Why is it essential for a Witch?
+ How do you (did you) choose your space?
+ What is your altar to you?

Chapter 3
INTRODUCING DEITY

These, then, are the unnamed gods, the forgotten gods, those who lay in the shadows of the many pantheons of humans. When you speak of the gods of nature, remember that nature is not only in human form—nor is the Divine. For there are gods far beyond those ever committed to paper or stone, whose names were never uttered by human throat nor drummed upon human ear.[22]

Whether you've come to this path because you feel you've made a strong connection to a deity (or deities), or you are feeling the distinct lack of any guiding consciousness in your spirituality, examining the notion of Deity is worth your time. There are many Witches who do not ascribe a personality to the energy they work wit—they often use the term "non-theistic Pagans" since the word "atheist" is so loaded with freight from the ongoing culture wars. However, there's a difference between having no communication with Deity and not

---

22. Lupa, "The Forgotten Gods of Nature," August 28, 2014. Accessed August 1, 2021. https://www.patheos.com/blogs/pathsthroughtheforests/2014/08/28/the-forgotten -gods-of-nature.

recognizing the messages when they are being sent to you. Likewise, a frequent conversation particularly with folks new to their spirituality is the constant questioning of occurrences in their environment and the omens they portend. Sometimes an unkindness of ravens is all over your car in the morning because somebody spilled popcorn, not because Apollo needs to have a word with you. What is important is to know what role Deity fulfills for those who do have such a belief; it is a role that typically needs to be filled within your own practice, even if you fill it with your own sense of self, the earth, or some other concept that carries no personification for you. How you think about this role will be one of the foundational principles of your practice.

Cultivating a relationship with the gods (note the plural), connecting to them through ritual, worshipping them through the cycle of the seasons, and honoring them through how we live our lives have traditionally been core aspects of being a Witch. As I said earlier, this role is foundational to your practice, and I don't advise removing Deity without understanding why you've done so or without knowing what you are inserting into their place. If a Witch does not have a connection with the gods, typically this is because they instead see themselves as connected more directly with nature or the egregore of all humanity. Then there is the middle ground—Witches who consider Deity as a metaphor for understanding primal energies rather than as entities unto themselves.

WHAT IS DEITY?

What is Deity, and how does it operate within our life? Anyone of any religion can love nature or direct energy, whether in prayer, consciousness-raising, or casting spells. Anyone of any religion can work with astrology, tarot cards, or crystals, or heal using energy or herbs. None of these things make a Witch. People have been doing these things long before Witchcraft existed. Cultivating a relationship with the gods (note the plural), connecting to them through ritual, worshiping them through the cycle of the seasons, and honoring them through how we live our life are core aspects of being a Witch. If a Witch does not have a connection with the gods, typically this is because they instead see themselves as connected more directly with nature, or with the egregore of all humanity. Then there is the middle ground—Witches who consider the gods metaphors for understanding primal energies rather than as entities unto themselves.

Typically, Witches believe that there are many deities, a distinct contrast to most other major world religions. Our deities come from many cultures and pantheons, but the most common amongst those with European ancestry are Greek, Roman, Norse, and the vast mélange of Celtic. Who we work with and worship may be based on our heritage (in my case, Celtic and Central European), or by need (such as working with White Tara to develop compassion), or even because they chose us (my deities are both Roman despite my having a limited cultural connection at best to Italy). The critical point is to work with the deities critical to you, not your friend, teacher, or what a book says to do. Likewise, a relationship with personified gods is something only you can come to; if your connection is to the energy that binds people together, it's not for me or anyone to tell you that you "should" call this energy Gaea, or Hòutǔ, or anything else. This connection is yours and yours alone, and just like any significant relationship, you want to treat it with respect.

Getting into a relationship with a deity is like getting into any relationship: parents, friends, lovers, acquaintances—all are entirely appropriate relationships one can have with Deity. Some Witches insist that Deity chooses you. Others (including myself way back in the day) choose based on need or desire. People's deities can come to them in dreams or rituals, sometimes resulting in the need to research and identify who it was. Still others have practiced Witchcraft for decades and, while they acknowledge the deities in their lives, have never had a formal relationship with any of them.

Being claimed by Deity is not necessarily desirable; it's not all kittens and garden walks. I made an offering to a deity a long time ago who was kind enough to recognize that I didn't know what I was doing. They did not accept that offering until years later when I *did* realize the enormity of the commitment. Part of that commitment is to go and do as they direct or be forsworn. This relationship has taken me to places and put me in situations I would never have sought on my own, and it will not cease until I leave this life. In working with them, I have been pushed out of my comfort zone, forced to burn away my self-delusions, and had my life wrecked on more than one occasion, all to force me to fix my problems and create a healthier person. The cosmic 2 x 4 has left a permanent dent in my head, and Deity wields it consistently with love and compassion, unyielding.

Each deity is a facet of an infinitely large and infinitely faceted diamond. Our relationship with that name or aspect allows us to begin to understand an infinitely large and complex power, the Divine. We recognize that working with a name or aspect limits the nature of the Divine, but without such a tool, we cannot begin to encompass the vastness that is the Divine.[23] In short, our cosmology is dual: narrow and infinite, personal and general.

Within that duality many of us see a further duality, that of gender. But while we recognize that the names and aspects are also labeled with opposite genders—Goddess and God, male and female—Deity is ultimately free of our socially conditioned images of male and female. The God and Goddess represent difference but are not themselves different. They are the same force flowing in opposite but not opposed directions. Neither is active or passive, dry or wet, dark or light. Each contains the other: Life breeds death, life feeds on death, death sustains life, making evolution and new creation possible. They are part of a cycle, each dependent on the other.

All religion is created by humankind, regardless of its inspiration, and we may use similar words and rituals. But unless every way you think is the same as mine, our religions are ultimately unique. My Witchcraft is not Daystar's, or Wren's, or John Q. Pagan's. This fierce individuality is reflected most strongly in how each of us will have our own nuanced concept of Deity, in our worship of Gaea, or the earth as a concept, or Apollo. The faces of Deity are different for each person even when we address them by the same name, and even the same image is seen differently from one person to another. Perception is never uniform, although the level of understanding may be. My perception may be female, or blond, or dark-skinned, or called "Jayne Dough," but it's *my* perception of Deity and my specific and personal spirituality; it doesn't need to mean anything to you.

For some, all deities are different faces of one singular being. "All gods are one god, all goddesses are one goddess, and there is one initiator."[24] Others see each name as a distinctly different being (Hermes is not Mercury is not Thoth, and so on.) These facets provide an excellent starting point as most of us think

---

23. Deity is not bothered by our inability to perceive their wholeness any more than a sighted person is when meeting someone blind.

24. Most often attributed to Dion Fortune in her *Aspects of Occultism* (Boston: Weiser, 2000), page number. Originally published 1962 by Aquarian Press (Northamptonshire, UK).

of Deity as god or goddess of something. One example is Nerrivik, the Inuit goddess of the sea and food at her most essential. If you were to work with her on a more personal level, you would come to understand that there are deeper layers to working with her and that being Inuit is a necessary component.

Deities are aspects of nature and human culture; it is by working with specific names or aspects that we form a more direct, intimate connection to them. As a starting point to beginning a relationship with Deity, you might list qualities that you admire, wish to create within yourself, or want to have in your life. Then look for deities who embody those qualities. Whoever you work with will bring their qualities into your life. My craft name (the special name Witches take and use only when they are being a Witch) is Maat; I chose it because I wanted to manifest many of the qualities of the Egyptian goddess Ma'at when leading ritual.[25]

MYTHOLOGY

Myths are the origin stories of Deity. They entertain, explain, and inform, providing context for why things are the way they are. Myth operates as a connection between the unknown and the known; a symbolic narrative describes ostensibly factual events of a deity. Myths capture universal psychic truths and influence our decisions, often subconsciously. When used within ritual, myths can bind a group together.

Campbell's Legacy

The experience, and therefore definition, of Deity varies through culture and time. I can only imagine that my numerously great ancestors had a much more direct relationship with Deity than I do. For them, Deity walked the earth and was involved in everyday interactions. Thunder wasn't molecules bouncing; it was the sound of a game played in the clouds or an angry voice. The killing of a deer was critical to the tribe's survival; the leader whose accurate dream of Deity telling them where to find the herd was a valuable resource. I don't need Deity to tell me where to find the nearest supermarket.

Joseph Campbell brought mythology, the origin stories of Deity, out of academia and children's books and into the homes of ordinary people. Let's also

---

25. My full craft name is longer than this but never shared in public; it remains a secret only Deity and a few initiates know.

take a moment to honor the work of Andrew Lang, who collected stories from many cultures and brought them into the homes of countless children over generations. Campbell believed that myths offer an enduring connection for all humans to the shared experiences of our lives.

Campbell's approach focused on finding the similarities within cultures, a complete reversal of previous scholars' work. He believed that re-examining primal characters and themes—e.g., the hero, death, resurrection, virgin birth, and promised land—could reveal our common psychological and spiritual roots: "Myths are the 'masks of God' through which men everywhere have sought to relate themselves to the wonders of existence."[26] Campbell sought to create a kind of unified field theory of Deity woven from myth, religion, psychology, science, and art. His writings profoundly influenced generations of creative artists and intellectuals.[27]

We Have to Talk About Jung

I'm not alone when I say that every Witch could benefit from studying the works of Carl G. Jung, the founder of analytical psychology. His concepts seem indispensable to a creative understanding of ourselves and other people. On a broader scale, his idea of the Collective Unconscious offers a key to psychic abilities, divination, and magic in general. Jung allowed for a direct and personal experience of Deity that did not require a psychological breakdown or religious framework. In so doing, he formed a picture where the existence of a superior entity, an organizing and a-causal principle (psychological or not) was evident and necessary.

Jung gave us language to describe and understand ourselves as beings with three distinct selves: an ego (our conscious self), subconscious (a personal memory bank we do not consciously access but may speak to us through dreams), and access to a Collective Unconscious made up of archetypes and complexes. Archetypes are "forms without content" that act as predispositions to behavior or potential patterns of behavior. Complexes can be positive or negative and form

---

26. Joseph Campbell, *The Hero's Journey: Joseph Campbell on His Life and Work*, 3rd Edition (Novato, CA: New World Library, 2003), xv.

27. If you are unfamiliar with Campbell's work, I urge you to view the series of conversations he filmed with Bill Moyers for PBS: https://billmoyers.com/content/ep-6-joseph-campbell-and-the-power-of-myth-masks-of-eternity-audio.

a cluster of components within the subconscious, influencing behavior and our decisions.

It's important to remember that Jung never talked about religion and faith; his concept of Deity is psychological, not religious. He believed that the idea of Deity originated from inner, psychological dynamics; whether Deity truly "exists" or not is entirely irrelevant.

> God is a psychic fact of immediate experience, otherwise there would never have been any talk of God. The fact is valid in itself, requiring no non-psychological proof and inaccessible to any form of non-psychological criticism. It can be the most immediate and hence the most real of experiences, which can be neither ridiculed nor disproved.[28]

In discussing Deity as a psychic fact, Jung includes other concepts such as the archetype of the Self (the totality and unity of opposites), synchronicity, and the collective unconscious. Together they formed a picture where the existence of a superior entity, an organizing, and a-causal principle, psychological or not, was evident and necessary.

The idea, question, and the concept of Deity is an anatomical fact for us, a part of our body just like the nervous system is an anatomical fact; we do not exist without it. If you shift your attention to your head, you don't theorize what it feels like to have a head; you immediately feel the fact of your head— the immediate reality of sensory feedback in every moment. You know you are a person who is seeking. It doesn't seem like much, this knowing, but that feeling of absolute knowledge is important to highlight. With that feeling as our bedrock, we can imagine there are many different faces or shadows or aspects of Deity (or the absolute). At the same time, we always recognize the difference between the *idea* of Deity, what we would like to believe about Deity, and the existence of reality.

---

28. While Jung referred exclusively to "God," his writings reveal that he clearly meant all genders and none. Quote from Carl Gustav Jung, *The Collected Works of C.G. Jung* (Princeton, NJ: Princeton University Press, 1953), 328..

GENDER, BIOLOGY, AND INCLUSIVITY

Traditionally, most versions of Witchcraft incorporate a dual-gendered Deity. The female encapsulated within the trilogy of Maiden-Mother-Crone, the male is either a counterpart or a dual-natured being splitting the solar year and ruling each half. These designations make sense in a nature-based spirituality in which the creative force follows the cycle of seasons and the seeding-growth-harvest-rest cycle of agriculture.

When we label some characteristics as "masculine" or "feminine," we lock ourselves into the dominant culture of self and other. Doing so limits our beliefs about what we are capable of becoming. Every quality is universal and available to the entire species—all humans have the capacity to nurture, abuse, discourse rationally, act emotionally, or pass judgment. If we enforce gender stereotypes, we ultimately disempower everyone. Coupling one's concept of a deity to biology is a human limitation; there is no reason to have only male or female deities.[29] Neither is there any reason to have only male-female mating and pairing. Instead of getting bound up in gender, it may be advantageous to see the traditional duality as different energies—projection and reception, creation and destruction—rather than male or female. Deity comes in every form and aspect. There are deities with no gender and those with more than one. Some deities have no sexual activity (such as Artemis), and others have partners of multiple genders (such as Hermes).

Right now, JaguarMoon is in the process of reviewing and revising its twenty years of ritual to expand our focus from only two genders. Our first steps were to stop using titles such as "High Priestess" and "High Priest"; instead, we say "Lead" and "Second" to allow any gender in those roles. We have found that we raise power, move, and have it accepted by Deity no matter the gender of the participants. We see this as a process taken with care and fully expect it will take many more years, but we are committed to creating an inclusive coven.

FINDING DEITY

For some, finding Deity (singular or plural) is not hard to do; they recognize or create a relationship effortlessly. I know some Witches who have been search-

---

29. I strongly recommend the work of LaSara Firefox Allen and her *Jailbreaking the Goddess* for more on the uncoupling of biology from Deity in the Witches' universe.

ing for years and still don't work with a specific deity. Others have given the subject due consideration and simply come to the conclusion that connection to personified Deity simply isn't for them. (Note that while I'm all for non-theistic Pagans, those who have dismissed Deity without doing the work of examining such a relationship are, in my opinion, walking through the world as if having never opened one of their eyes.) Many Witches will work with a name for a single ritual and no further. Think of this as a very respectful and consensual one-night stand. It's good for both sides, and everyone leaves feeling good. Creating a longer-term relationship will require more effort, just like any partnership.

Do your research and look for parts of Deity's story that resonate with you. My friend Jeannine is a blacksmith and immediately felt a connection to Brigit, goddess of smithcraft, poetry, and healing. LJ is an orphan and adoptee and recognized his story unexpectedly in the mythology of Anubis. Once your interest is piqued, start looking for signs that the deity is interested in you. These signs might come in the form of suddenly seeing symbols personal to the deity (e.g., keys for Hecate or holly for Baldur) that you never noticed before or hearing music that reminds you of them. Perhaps the deity will show up in your dreams or send messengers into your life, such as animals sacred to them. Meditate, pray, and journal—these will lead you deeper into understanding who might be asking for a relationship.

It is never a bad idea to read mythology; deity origin stories often provide fodder for connecting with your own life. All religions have their origins in mythology, and every culture has myths and stories that define them. Mythology and scholarly research will lead you to understand what sort of things they like and if there is a specific time, day, season, or lunar phase closely associated with them. What do they value? Remember: don't just accept a single point of information or one that can't point to source material. Too many websites repeat the same information without providing valid references, which is how you can end up thinking that Hecate is a maiden goddess![30]

Not every deity who shows up is going to be a long-term commitment. Some just want attention for a short time or a specific task. My longtime magical partner, Daystar, has had a whole procession of deities come through his

---

30. While Hecate is occasionally shown dressed in a maiden's skirt on Greek vases, that is the extent of any association of her as a maiden.

life in the decades we have worked together. Each has a message for him or someone in his life or a specific task to accomplish. Some stayed for just a day, others for weeks or even months. Through it all, his primary deity pair (Hera and Pan) remain constant.

Nor is every odd thing that happens in your life a sign that someone wants your attention. (This is why you keep a Book of Shadows , noting what is and isn't especially odd.) A good baseline is to look for strange or unusual things that come in threes. If you actively look for signs of a relationship, you might try telling the deity that you need the signs to be clear and in threes. A mistake I often see new students make is to see signs in *every* out-of-the-ordinary thing that happens to them without otherwise tracking occurrences. If they were able to keep a detailed record of every single moment of their life, it would quickly become clear how the unusual is ordinary. It is the repetition of unusual things that make them potentially noteworthy.

Once you think you have a connection, figure out how to work with and worship them. This relationship is a partnership—you both get something out of it, and it will require time and attention, like any relationship. Plan a ritual to acknowledge the relationship formally, explaining why you want to work with them or accept their overture to work with you.

This portion of the lesson gives you some tools to find a deity if you don't already have one. Nonetheless, please keep in mind two things:

1. It is not necessary to have a relationship with a deity to be a Witch.
2. You have a choice in accepting a deity's overture! If you feel a deity is scary or distasteful, respectfully say, no thanks or not yet. If the being doesn't leave you alone, start questioning whether they are genuinely divine or just a malignant entity out to cause trouble. (This is a highly unusual occurrence but if it happens to you, end the contact immediately. Carefully close your circle and cleanse your space before using it again.)

If you have decided to work with a specific deity, it's best to start simple. Pick a culture that interests you and read its myths.[31] As you learn about the various cultures and deities, keep track of which stories interest you, catch your

---

31. Check the sources; some so-called encyclopedic entries are not based on cultural writing.

eye, or otherwise linger in your mind. Likewise, track the deities who catch your eye. Read their stories and note who they interact with, and how. Try not to get frustrated if this takes a long time to do. Part of the value of research is discovering things that will help you to understand the beliefs of others better, even if you do not choose to use the knowledge.

Let's Talk About Cultural Appropriation and Erasure

Learning about another culture isn't cultural appropriation, using something out of context for its roots, without respect for its place within a larger cultural practice is the problem. Similarly, adopting a practice that removes resources or sovereignty from the original culture is a problem. Growing your own white sage (*Salvia apiana*, the most commonly used herb for burning to cleanse one's environment, often called smudging) for use in your own rituals is perfectly acceptable, buying it from a place that isn't ethically sourcing it, is a problem. As a seeker, it is extra difficult to discern when you may be crossing a boundary; who do you trust?

When stepping outside your culture of origin, ask yourself:

+ Am I excited by this person/object/practice because it's exotic, or can I see the commonality between us?
+ Can I participate in this (non-white-origin) practice with the full knowledge that my ancestors were engaged in actions that actively harmed the people from whom this practice comes?
+ Have I been invited by a non-white person to partake in this practice?

We all came from the same ancestors. To my mind, that means that there is no practice that cannot be learned. Yet, to do so without understanding its place within the larger cultural landscape is a bad idea, one that will lead to negative consequences.[32]

To understand the gods and how our ancestors worshipped, you must understand their culture of origin. Far too often, a new Witch will take on smudging, for example, based on a fun crafts project they saw online without ever understanding why indigenous peoples believe it works in the first place. As these cultures struggle even to survive, not acknowledging the unique

---

32. A source I highly recommend on this topic is *Talking About the Elephant*, edited by Lupa.

traditions that make them what they are simply hastens their demise. As an exercise, briefly consider Italian culture. Note the first five things you think of. Now try to imagine that you gave credit for those things to the people of the American Midwest. Try it again: think about Italy and note the next five things that come to mind. Now give credit for those things to the people of Nova Scotia. Repeated again and again, eventually (if not already) you're going to have a hard time thinking of anything distinctly Italian. Now imagining those things you thought were never distinctly Italian, what kind of impression do you even have of Italians? Mightn't you even ask what the point of Italy even is? They seem to just be southern Switzerland, after all.

When considering a deity, look for material that tells you about that specific culture and time and the deity in question. Choosing the goddess Kali Ma, for example, would at a minimum necessitate that you learn as much as you can about the various cultures of India, as well as Kali Ma's sects in particular. Ask yourself: Why is she worshipped as she is, and why did specific cults grow up around her? What prompted the type of worship that her followers practice? What were some of the political problems that gave rise to making her powerful? Explore the ancient texts of the culture and their various religions to understand the deity's place in the scheme of things. If you find your own culture isn't working, feel free to look at others. Right now, you are merely attempting to find out what might work for you, so don't limit yourself too much.

Take copious notes as you go and arrange them into some sort of notebook for later use so the details are not lost. When you think you've finished with one, go on to another until you've exhausted your list. More than likely, you will add to your list as you go. Pay particular attention to the things associated with them: animals, plants, trees, colors, gems, or scents. (These will help you build ritual practices in their honor when the time comes.)

In some cases, you will have to make educated guesses. For example, Diana is the Roman goddess of the hunt, as well as the moon. Her symbols include wild animals (bear, deer, wolf, etc.), hunting gear (primarily bow, quiver, and arrows), and the moon. She is unmarried, and thus is a maiden, making the waxing crescent moon and the season of spring particularly important to her. She is a twin, giving her guardianship of childbirth and fertility. When choosing stones, those associated with the moon and weapons are most precious to her (silver, iron, pearl, quartz, diamond, and moonstone). For colors, look to those found in the forest and the night sky. Scents for anointing or incense would also be best drawn from the forest and the night: jasmine, pine, anemone, and rosemary.

I can't stress enough the importance of considering how much you know about any culture you are considering researching further. Do you have any connection to its traditions in your life? Nothing says that you are absolutely forbidden from working with deities from a culture you aren't genetically tied to, but you risk those deities not welcoming you. When approaching a new culture, begin with humility: assume you are starting from zero and concentrate on learning as much as possible for it to take hold.

Deity Engineering Worksheet

The following worksheet can guide you to finding a deity. I based it on one initially created by Amber K.[33]

1. What qualities do you most need in your life right now? (They can be emotional, physical, or mental qualities.)

2. What makes you feel most out of control or helpless?

3. What qualities or aspects of life make you feel good, robust, secure, and healthy?

4. When you think of Deity, what abilities or powers do you think they might have?

5. When you think of Deity, do you sense specific physical qualities? (Hair, skin, or eye color are the most common, but age, gender, and clothing can be relevant.)

6. Does the deity have any jewels, weapons, or other objects associated with them?

7. Does the deity have a specific space or place that is sacred to them?

8. What unique relationships does this deity have to other deities, creatures, or humans?

---

33. From my Book of Shadows. Amber K's worksheet was published in 1990 at "EARTH RITE," attributed as "Courtesy of Amber K." It can be found various places online with no further attribution.

Getting to Know Deity

When you have a tentative list of deities that you want to know better, move to the next step. Make a list of your skills and knowledge. You might list what you are moving towards on your life's path or desire to bring into your life. Do any of the deities on your list complement those? If so, start there.

Pick one deity and take your notes to your quiet place. Take some incense and a candle that you think might be appropriate to them.[34] If you don't like burning things or have a problem with smells (I sympathize) try using essential oils or instrumental music that feels appropriate. Cast a circle around the area you are in and then center yourself.

Examine your notes on the deity and hold their qualities and attributes in your mind as you light the incense. The incense should help you meditate as well as be something appropriate to offer to that specific deity. Spend some time reaching out to this deity and remember what comes to your mind. Sometimes the deity will give you a message, and sometimes they are silent. The critical part of this process is to see if the two of you want to work together. It may take a single session or several; give it the time needed. When you feel done, blow out the candle and thank the deity. Let the incense burn out on its own. Release your circle and make notes about what happened, how it felt, and what you think. Repeat this exercise until you believe you have found enough for now and can make a closer connection with the ones chosen.

My favorite explanation is that Deity *is*. (Similarly, I also like the scene in the movie *Dogma* where the Apostle jumps up from his seat, levels two fingers at the Bishop, and cries aloud "… He that is I AM!") [35]

Atheistic/Nontheistic Witchcraft

I've called this out several times, but let's dig into this concept for a moment. You may have diligently gone through this chapter, you've done the exercises, and your consistent answer to all of it is "sorry, I'm not feeling any of this." Years ago, my answer to you might have been to keep trying, it'll come eventually, but as I've encountered more and more Witches and pagans, I've come to understand that there is a place in this world for the spiritualist, the energy worker,

---

34. In my experience, sandalwood and a white candle are always appropriate.

35. *Dogma*, dir. Kevin Smith, Santa Monica, CA: Lionsgate Films, 1999.

the ritualist… whatever you want to call them, who practices everything I do but never puts name to the energy that they work with. It's a perfectly valid framework.

For the nontheistic Witch the idea of moving energy, connecting with others, and performing magic and rituals sits comfortably, but they have simply never felt a personified mind behind any of these workings.[36] They hear the stories others tell of the first time the Goddess laid her hand upon them and think, "that sounds really interesting; it's never happened to me, though." Too many of these Witches are made to feel like they aren't "real" Witches yet, but don't worry, you'll get there some day! Instead, the nontheistic Witch should be considered as simply having a different relationship with energy than others. If you need to see it within a deity framework, consider "nature" to be the voice that the Goddess has chosen to speak in; as I've said repeatedly, everyone's relationship with Deity is unique to them. However, while this may help you to grasp nontheistic Witchcraft if you are someone who does work with personified Deity, remember that this revisioning of yours is only for your own benefit; your nontheistic friend doesn't see it this way and won't take kindly to you telling them that they just haven't sorted it out yet.

The only serious danger the nontheistic Witch faces is if they are claiming non-theism because they want to avoid the possibility of experiencing Deity. If they actually do live in a world of deities reaching out to them but shun these personified gods while still wanting to do their magic, eventually they are going to have a really bad time with it. Nobody likes to be taken advantage of, and deities are notoriously jealous and proud. If you're doing a lot of water magic, and Poseidon has been calling out to you each and every time and you're turning deaf ears to him, he is going to make his displeasure known. However, it is also quite possible that you're doing your water magic and the only thing calling out to you is the water. If so, no harm done.

Activity

Name at least five aspects of a deity. For each aspect, provide at least one name and several ways that aspect is different from other ones.

---

36. A phrase that gets used for much the same reason that people will rename one or the other side of the pro-life/pro-choice argument; "atheist" carries a lot of freight in some circles and these Witches don't want to be unfairly burdened with it.

Contemplate your most potent/profound/moving spiritual experience. It does not have to be religious in nature; the decision about what you believe is powerful and spiritual is up to you.

In your Book of Shadows, answer these questions:

+ Who are the gods?
+ Are the gods "real" or a product of the imagination? A psychological construct?
+ What part does mythology play in bringing us closer to Deity?
+ Do you feel an affinity for a particular deity? Who, and why? Share the story of how you two "met."

If you do not feel an affinity, complete the Deity Engineering Worksheet from earlier. Start researching pantheons and see if anyone calls to you.

1. Make a list of the characteristics you feel most represent the deity you honor and revere.
2. To get an idea of which pantheon may be "yours," think about the culture you most admire or forms your DNA. Are your roots Norse? Japanese? Native American? Greek? Each of these cultures has ancient, diverse pantheons. Read all the names of the deities. Read the descriptions of the names. Do any match your list from question one? Which ones? Partially?
3. Write out or draw the family tree of the pantheon you chose. (For example, with the Greek pantheon, start with the Titans and then Zeus, his sister/wife Hera, their siblings, children, etc.)

Bonus Materials

You may enjoy the chapter "Myths and Mythology," excerpted from Bryan S. Rennie's *Reconstructing Eliade: Making Sense of Religion*, at http://mjoseph. comminfo.rutgers.edu/rennie.html.

Chapter 4
WHAT IS MAGIC?

Magic isn't the empty parroting of words and actions; it is an involved, emotionally charged experience in which the words and actions are used as focal points or keys to unlock the power that we all possess.[37]

In the introduction, I described the difference between *magic* and *magick* in a notational sense, but it begs the question: what is magic? Magic is alive within and all around you; you don't need to believe in it; it never goes away. In Witchcraft, one way we see the Universe is as being composed of energy. Whether solids, liquids, or gas, the form does not matter; it is all microscopic particles held together at the sub-atomic level by energy. Proven by modern science, this view of the Universe is thousands of years old, as we see from the teachings of the Vedic sages in India. Energy is not static; it is responsive and dynamic with movements that mimic fluid—but comparisons are limited in providing explanation. Rather than just reading about it, working with energy gives the best understanding.

We interact with energy every day, albeit unconsciously; it takes its shape from us, reacting instantly and as naturally as air conforming to the earth's

---

37. Commonly attributed to Scott Cunningham.

surface or water to the seafloor. However, when we consciously interact with energy, bringing our intellect and—most importantly—our will to bear, we create magic. Magic is the art of consciously focusing and controlling the energy of the Universe.

To effect change, we must move beyond petty desires and the gadfly of our id, our younger self. That self is interested in satisfying wants and desires. Like a magpie, it is distracted by any new, shiny object. It is a deep source of power, a pool of energy connected directly to the primal elements of the world. Younger self controls our instinctive behavior and understands movement, music, ritual, rhyme, water, stars, and shiny things. To impress younger self, we need to get its attention through tricks. It likes simple rhymes and soothing or repetitive music. Candles and incense get its attention and tell it that what we're about to do is important and interesting. While we are fascinating our younger self, we must reach out to our higher self—the best in us—our connection to the Divine so that our natural passions align with that which sees further and broader than we can. Regular meditation and mental exercises aid this connection. When we do magic, we raise energy, focus it on the desired outcome, and then direct that energy to manifest our will. For newcomers it can feel impossible, but I assure you it is only difficult and gets easier with practice. Working magic requires a change in consciousness, often aided by external factors and symbols. Through magic, we influence or control the world around us; it is a tremendous responsibility that requires a high standard of morality.

Magic also requires work. You can cast a "perfect" spell, but it will go to naught if you don't back it up in the physical realm. Magic is the blueprint; it's up to you to build the structure that allows your will to manifest. If you run into trouble or experience unintended consequences, go back to that blueprint and take a look at what you were working for—maybe you got precisely what you asked for (as opposed to what you wanted)? We live in a multi-dimensional Universe, and it's difficult for us to think beyond three dimensions, so it's less of a surprise that the spell didn't work as it is that any spell *does* work!

One way to think about how magic works is this: every action, thought, and emotion broadcasts and connects into the collective unconsciousness. This connection powers our magic. Everyone feels it differently; my definition is not yours, nor is yours likely the same as your friend's, and when we lose the connection, we feel confused and lonely.

Magic is like a coin—you only see one side of it. But working with energy and magic teaches us to acknowledge the reality of the parts we can't see. The entire object has an existence on its own, but it also inhabits a realm we cannot see. If belief is the primary tool in Witchcraft, then Will is the engine that powers it.

If your physical reality is a mess, it will be exponentially more difficult to manifest your will. The saying "be careful what you wish for" applies here. For example, if you find yourself short of cash, you might say, "I want to pay all my bills by the end of this month." Sounds like the right solution, doesn't it? But what if what comes to you is a part-time job that sucks up all of your free time, and getting your bills paid messes up your relationship with your lover?

Our ancestors believed that there were people who had the unique ability to affect the physical world. These people were likely the first priests or shamans and came from all genders; their "unique ability" was their aptitude for getting in touch with magic. It would have to be intuitive for them, since at first there wouldn't have been anyone to share information with. They could protect the community and its individuals from harm, whether by sensing the presence of game to feed their tribe, reading the weather and so able to plant and reap at the best times, or able to detect the "demons" of mental illness and cure them. These people were valuable to a community dependent on living in close harmony with the natural world.

With the rise of technology and formal religions, these wise ones were marginalized and eventually hunted down. After the Inquisition, Witchcraft and other "alternative" spiritualities went into hiding or were lost, but the belief in magic clearly continued. In the late 1800s, several magical lodges dedicated to various forms of ceremonial magic formed and pushed the idea of magic into the public light. Magic was redefined as the art of changing consciousness at will, shifting it from a perspective of working in harmony with nature to one of control over it. It marked a profound shift from the ancient model: sovereign beings of power, once seen as conscious entities of vast might, became barely more than pale imaginings subservient to the ego. Magic was stripped of its primordial power, reduced to categorization and lists. Marketing gave us labels for different kinds of Witches, each with their own box so that newcomers could know what to do without effort or research. Under this model, spells became recipes: put the ingredients in a bowl, stir, and say these words for love, work stress, a new bike. No need for Deity, no need for anything other than these ingredients. It even works a lot of the time.

Witchcraft is about connection. It is the feeling that you get when you stand in the presence of the Divine, when you acknowledge the power of nature and our relationship to the Universe, when you feel/see how you are the same as the butterfly, the stone, the fish, the apple, the wolf. I like what Deborah Blake says, "Witchcraft is sensing what you shouldn't be able to sense … [It] is intuition on overdrive, faith in the face of overwhelming reality, and applying the force of your will to change that reality into something better."[38]

Underlying the appearance of solidity and separateness is a constantly changing vortex of moving forces, currents of energy that dissolve and re-form endlessly. Seeing this world requires a shift away from ordinary consciousness into an extraordinary mode. In waking this mode within ourselves, what Starhawk poetically calls "starlight vision," we must be willing to step outside of the mainstream and become somewhat alienated from our culture.[39]

We also understand the difference between magic and psychosis, a distinction that lies in maintaining the ability to step back, at will, into ordinary consciousness. Flying is effortless in the astral, but here in the physical, it will likely end in injury (unless you're doing it in a plane).

Magic assumes the presence of subtle energies. What scientists call visible light—the entire rainbow of radiation observable to the human eye—is only about 0.0035 percent of the electromagnetic spectrum, yet what we cannot see (such as X-rays and ultraviolet light) still affects us. Similarly, magic is about focusing on non-physical energies and directing them to create change. When we engage in meditation, breath control, voice work, bodywork, visualization, and ritual, we improve our body and mind. Those acts sharpen and balance us, enabling us to perceive and wield more subtle energies. Your magic is as strong as your will; the more balanced and integrated you are, the stronger your will.

Possibly the most significant difference between a Witch's magic and many religions is that working magic places emphasis on ourselves to work for change. There are no gurus in magic, there are only fellow students with dif-

---

38. Deborah Blake, *Witchcraft on a Shoestring: Practicing the Craft Without Breaking Your Budget* (Woodbury, MN: Llewellyn Publications,, 2010), 198.

39. Starhawk, *The Spiral Dance: A Rebirth of the Ancient Religions of the Great Goddess*, 20th *Anniversary edition* (San Francisco: Harper Collins, 1999), 42.

ferent perspectives and experiences. In other words, whereas in many faiths it is the role of the general participant to appeal either to their temporal leader or to their deity and then wait for the results of that higher authority's effort, working magic places you as the fulcrum of achievement. *You* leverage your will upon your intent in order to move the world.

Magic tends to work primarily with symbols, the language of the unconscious. Symbols can be a powerful source as they have many functions; one of these, released through magic, can be the ability to confound the ego and the internal censor, enabling us to perceive more subtle truths or experience direct revelations. Although we may not be able to explain precisely how symbols work, we know from experience that certain symbols seem harmonious with certain types of energy. For example, a magician may tell you that if you want to attract love, the correct procedure is to wear green and apply rose perfume, and perhaps keep copper on you such as a bracelet or necklace. These are all symbols attributed to Venus, who is associated with love. Our magic links our desire for love with that of a deity charmed by our offerings, and we are thus granted our wish. This form of magic, sympathetic magic or contagion (an odd-sounding term for sure, explained later in this chapter), is one of the most commonly practiced and the oldest.

Magic can be a painful process. It is not easy to maintain the discipline and honest self-critical approach all the time. It can also be hard work dealing with the energy released without being knocked off balance sometimes. The important thing in these cases is to remain honest and keep at it.

MAGIC IS POWER

Magic is not a religion, spirituality, or prayer; those are all based on faith and the presence of an external force. We might believe that the Divine blesses or gifts us with magic and might offer worship in return. However, when we do magic, we are taking on the mantle of Deity. "The wise magician aspires to the power of a god all the while knowing that he or she is not God."[40]

One can be a Witch and never work magic. If we choose to work magic, however, we are seeking power with the intent to use it to deliberately alter our world in alignment with our will. Magic (and spellcraft, how Witches manifest their

---

40. Sophie Reichter, *Spiritual Protection: A Safety Manual for Energy Workers, Healers, and Psychics*, (Newburyport, MA: Red Wheel/Weiser, 2018), 200.

magic) is spiritual power. If you want to do magic, you are saying to the universe that you are ready and willing to access the cosmic power plant and use its energy to effect change. Magic is both a science and an art—using it begins with disciplining our mind to focus our will. As we do so, we are transformed.

Just as with any kind of power, using magical power requires respect and knowledge. I'm perfectly happy to replace a light with a ceiling fan, but I make sure to wear rubber-soled shoes and disconnect the electricity first. In a similar manner, magic can cause an accident if not properly prepared for and controlled. Respect magic. While there is nothing wrong with having a playful and fun attitude when exploring magic, seeing magic only as a game trivializes it and causes us to miss out on its best aspects.

Magic requires change and transformation. In choosing to use it, we must shed the blinders of conventional thinking and cultural indoctrination. We must dig out the essential truths hidden deep within us to seek what lies outside the confines of mass consciousness. A Witch lives in the liminal, on the fringes of established paradigms.

Witches do not accept things as they are. We look with discerning eyes and deep awareness of what is and work to make it better. We ask, "what if?" and begin to see what is needed. We realize that others cling to illusions like a child clings to its blanket and choose to make different choices. When we think for ourselves and make decisions based on awareness and a desire for change, we move outside of society.

Magic requires consciousness. Magic requires awareness. Magic requires Will.

TWO RULES

Many of us come to Witchcraft with a desire to work magic. The rent is due and there's not enough to pay it; work is dragging and you've got to make a change. Spellwork can usually happen quickly using commonly found ingredients, making it very attractive when we need a quick fix. I completely respect that need. That said, there are two rules to follow.

1. Plan your magic carefully.
2. Know yourself.

As a beginner everything will take longer, but starting with good habits will always prepare you better for the long run. You may want to create an actual checklist, at least at first. If so, your list would include:

+ What exactly do you want to accomplish? This is your true goal, the linchpin of the spell.

+ Will achieving your goal cause harm to another, in any way? While I don't follow the ethic of the rede's "harm none" statement, I strongly do not recommend working against another. We so rarely can see the true effects of our magic, especially as newcomers to Witchcraft, why deliberately cause harm if there are other solutions?

+ What symbols and props support your intention? This is why others' spells are so rarely useful. Each of us creates a personal language; we need to use symbols that are meaningful to us, not some writer. Green might be the color of money for many people in the United States but not for people in Great Britain.

+ Is there a timeframe you want to follow? Some spells are best done in specific times of the month, a season, or over a period of time.

+ How will you know you succeeded? No spell is meant to be forever; you may need to stop even if you haven't succeeded.

The above list is just a beginning; I promise that planning will get easier as you learn more. I also promise that you will take a lifetime to know yourself, the most difficult aspect of working with power. The work we do with meditation is a large part of how we come to know ourselves so well we can do magic without worry. Coming to understand and acknowledge our true selves is the practice of a lifetime. Magic is fun and exciting, so our egos can easily get caught up in the excitement at the expense of common sense. Working magic instead of going through ordinary effort is a poor use of your resources, and will backfire (spectacularly!) eventually. Moreover, no spell works well without mundane support. I can visualize and craft a spell for a new job, but if I never send a resume or network with my contacts, that job will not materialize.

Magic empowers us to make change in our lives and in doing so brings about positive change within us.

THE COLORS OF MAGIC?

Many newcomers to Witchcraft think there are three kinds of magic: white, gray, and black. White magic is the good kind, they say, the kind where no one gets hurt and you are a being of Light interested primarily in furthering your spiritual growth. Gray magic is a little sketchy, if only because you ask for something for yourself, like getting a better job or attracting a lover. Black magic is scary and *bad*, the magic of manipulation and harm, interfering with another's free will.

The black-versus-white magic divide is arbitrary, culturally specific, and rooted in the dogma of the faith many of us were raised in but left behind. Magic is like any tool: it can harm or heal. We talk about magic being energy, so think of it as electricity: when used to power your home, it's beneficial; stick your hand in a socket and you could die. Same power, different effects. Moreover, the words *black* and *white* have implicit racial bias and shouldn't be used to describe morality all. I mean, really. Why are dark things also bad/negative? Why is light/white better? Time to move beyond the duality.

Of course, magical actions can have severe consequences, and most of us would agree that some types of magic are cruel and destructive. But that is more about an individual Witch's ethics than a societal judgment. Magic is open to anyone, as long as they are willing to do the work of cleansing before, clearing during, and handling the outcome after. I can't tell you how many times I've heard a Witch ask, "how did that happen?" often followed by a thoughtful "I should have seen that coming."

Magic doesn't look or feel the same for everyone. It depends on your culture, your lifestyle, your home environment, your interest, your abilities, and your passions. And this is the key: it's your magic.

Activity

Journal in your Book of Shadows about whether you want to work magic or not. If so, what you would do if you knew your magic would work 100 percent of the time. What would you change in your life? In the world?

Spend a day noting the moments that make you feel something. When you do, stop and take notice. Write it in your Book of Shadows (later, if the moment isn't convenient). Doing so prepares the ground for connections to happen more frequently.

Chapter 5
ETHICS OF THE WITCH

The ethical man knows it is wrong to cheat on his wife, whereas the moral man actually wouldn't.[41]

Ethics are a core part of being a human within the world; without them, we would not have society. Ethics are for individuals, morals come to us from our culture, and laws provide a standardized, enforceable guideline for the larger group we exist within. For the spiritual person, ethics are the decisions we make in daily life, morals are how society expects us to behave, and it is all enclosed within a ring of divine law. This last ring could be called karma but is more easily described as *the things we do not do because they would offend Deity*.

Having a coherent system of ethics is a defining characteristic of any religion, but I refuse to give you the Witch's equivalent of the Ten Commandments! Instead, consciously think about and forge your perspective from which to navigate life. An essential part of a Witch's development comes when they

---

41. Ducky, from the TV show *NCIS* (Donald Bellisario, Don McGill, and Steven D. Binder, "Escaped" *NCIS*, season 4, episode 2. NBC, September 26, 2006.)

consciously create a set of ethical guidelines, taking responsibility for the consequences of their actions.

THE REDE

These eight words the Wiccan rede fulfill;
An it harm none, do what ye will.

Any newcomer to the Craft gets told or reads that all Witches follow the Rede, usually presented as either "harm none" or "an it harm none, do what ye will." An online search using the term "Rede" returns more than 500,000 results; any website offering information about the "basics of Witchcraft" will include the Rede, and pretty much any book about Witchcraft discusses it, even if only briefly. The Rede seems to be a foundational principle of the Craft. But it wasn't always.

Before the mid-1970s in the United States, the Rede was virtually unknown.[42] Around that time, Witches began to explore magic outside of covens, aided by the works of Buckland, Cunningham, and Starhawk. These authors all proffered a form of Witchcraft called Wicca that focused on creating a solitary practice, opening up a formerly closed practice to anyone with the ability to buy a book. Buckland, for example, wrote:

> What I set out to do is create a modern form of Wicca…I felt a need to make it a more democratic form for covens, so that no one could get into an uncontrollable position of power. I also wanted it to be available to both single (Solitary) Witches as well as groups (covens). And lastly, I wanted it to be something that anyone could enter without having to seek out an already established group and without having to submit to their rules and regulations.[43]

The increasing number of solitaires and eclectics led directly to a considerable increase in the number of people researching (and practicing) Witchcraft

---

42. My thanks to Shea Thomas of the Wiccan Rede Project Resurrection for doing the research on the Rede's origins. Accessed September 28, 2020. https://www.gocek.org/pagan/wiccanredeproject.

43. Raymond Buckland, "Introduction to the 2005 Edition", *Buckland's Book of Saxon Witchcraft* (Boston: Weiser Books, 2005), iv.

on their own. They were searching for and relying upon any sources of information they could find. So, it becomes conceivable that this new generation of Witches adopted the Rede and made it a central part of their practice in a way that might never have happened if they had stayed within the traditional coven model. Indeed, the rising popularity of Witchcraft and the increasing numbers of people practicing it led to an explosion of media interest. Thus, the Rede also became the "go-to" ethical statement and sound bite to explain what a Witch believes.

Do We Need the Rede?

The Rede is, of course, just one version of the many creeds, codes, and rules that fall under the umbrella of "Golden rules" that include many sayings familiar to most of us: Hippocrates cautioned doctors to, "first, do no harm." Aristotle said, "We should conduct ourselves toward others as we would have them act toward us." Confucius proclaimed, "Do unto another what you would have him do unto you, and do not do unto another what you would not have him do unto you. Thou needest this law alone. It is the foundation of all the rest." In the Talmud, it says, "If I am not for myself, who will be for me? If I am not for others, who am I for? And if not now, when?" Even St. Augustine proclaimed, "Love, and do what you like."

Much like the atheists' view that they do not need the threatened revenge of a spirit in the sky or a pit of flame after death in order to be moral, Witches don't need eight words to decide right or wrong. (Significantly, the founder of Wicca's injunction of "do no harm" referred explicitly to the use of magic and not general behavior.)

Keep in mind that most of us have lived in a society of power-over and domination for thousands of years, one in which power flows from the top down while responsibility flows from the bottom up. This kind of power structure requires the support of social and legal measures to ensure a controlled populace, particularly in their private practices. If people begin to think for themselves, they may not conform to controlling strictures. New ways of thinking could produce new ways of living.

Witches defy control. Instead of blindly obeying societal norms, we choose the much more difficult path of personal responsibility for all of our actions, failures, and successes. We do not mouth words of law while engaging in irresponsible behavior. Rather, we choose to take whatever steps necessary to contribute to personal growth in a positive manner.

To my mind, if an ethical structure is going to hold, it must survive the test of time and temptation. Being told what "right" or "wrong" is has to pass my standards—society has gotten it wrong too many times.[44] People need to understand what constitutes "right" to avoid the wrong; it's something they need to figure out for themselves.

For each of us, that growth will be different—my need to stop being so critical is not your need to express anger. We all have difficult personal choices to make and hard decisions to follow. It is so much simpler if all aspects of our lives are regulated, with the rules and regulations written down, and all guidance comes from authority: no more thinking, no hard choices, no more struggling over ethical conflicts. However, if we are all doing the work, we will likely act in harmony with the larger society.

Ethics and Magic

As we begin our path, it seems like a good idea to consciously develop a set of personal ethics that maintains respect for those of the community in which we exist. Do some soul searching and decide how you feel about things. Question your teachers and what you are learning; your sense of ethics and morals will evolve.

Deliberately creating one's ethics requires honesty—complete, objective, and total honesty with yourself. This level of honesty cannot be brutal or harsh; it's not a punishment. But few of us were raised with sufficient objectivity. As children, we learned that being "good" meant pleasing our parents, who punished us when we failed. However, by becoming Witches we move away from societal standards and into fresh territory. Honesty and objectivity are our tools, not punishment.

Once we learn to look objectively at ourselves and the world around us, we begin to understand cause and effect and start to judge the value of our endeavors accurately. With understanding comes the wisdom that we cannot change others but can change ourselves and our reactions. Understanding does not mean agreement: I can understand *why* a person beats a child without in

---

44. For example, the people who hid Anne Frank and her family in WWII-era Netherlands were breaking the law; the people who killed her were following the law.

any way condoning it. Yet, having discovered the situation, I have an ethical choice about how I want to react to the knowledge. Do I call the authorities and have the child removed from danger? Do nothing and allow the beating to continue? Do I befriend the person and try to get them to counseling? Find another solution?

Exploring our ethics begins with honesty and a willingness to face the truth. Having done so, we must also be willing to act on that truth, knowing we will never know everything before making decisions. Therefore, we will make mistakes. We will have to learn from those mistakes and change our minds and actions. We must also be willing to forgive ourselves.

Rarely will the ethical choices we make be life-or-death. Instead, they will be countless tiny decisions that seem to have nothing to do with ethics. Do I wear a blue or white shirt today? Can I walk the dog early or put her off until after dinner? Take the bus, or drive the car to get groceries? Tiny choices, small decisions; they seemingly having nothing to do with ethics at all. However, each decision provides us with countless opportunities to make *conscious* decisions. These are opportunities to think honestly, consciously, and objectively about the situation before deciding what to do.

The Rede is not a commandment. It is an ethical philosophy providing a way to measure actions through the lens of personal responsibility. Witchcraft offers a spiritual practice that values every individual's intrinsic value and right to self-determination.

Activity

Consider your own ethics. Do you know where you've drawn your own lines and how you are acting "right" within the world? Explore this in your Book of Shadows. Where are you tempted to violate your precepts and why?

Journal about the ethics of being a Witch. How might these ethics be different from what you have learned from your culture? How are they different from your family of origin?

Journal your answers to the following:

+ What is honesty?
+ I am most likely to be dishonest when …
+ List your ten best character traits.

+ List no more than three things about yourself that you would change.
+ Think about the concept of "perfect love, perfect trust": What does it mean to you?
+ What does the Rede mean to you? How do you live it?

There are a series of ethical dilemmas posted on my website. Choose three that produce a strong response—positive or negative—in you. Journal about how you would handle them.

Bonus Materials: *Maat's System of Ethics*

When I first created this lesson, I also created a system of ethics. It took ages…and it's also evolved. My system originally included dozens of rules, then only three; I kept finding reasons to add and remove rules based on various imagined scenarios. In the end, however, what resulted was a system I abide by and revisit annually. Here is my system, with commentary.

1. *An it harm none, do what you will.* My starting point and generally a good way of going through the world. That said, I acknowledge there are times when deliberately creating harm is necessary, making this rule one that requires constant evaluation.

2. *Never speak falsehood.* Incredibly difficult, mainly since my mundane job is in management, and there are times when I must carefully weigh my obligations.

3. *Be cautious when withholding the truth.* Withholding information is always potentially a lie and requires a significant moral decision each time the situation arises. I base my navigation on two principles:

   + Am I withholding the truth because it is easier on me? My decision can't be to save myself discomfort (e.g., little "harmless" lies).
   + Will it do them harm if they do or do not know what I am withholding? The decision must always focus on the needs of the person from whom I'm withholding the truth.
   + The assessment of another's needs is a complex dynamic of power-over and responsibility. Moreover, it requires acknowledgment that we tend to underestimate the capacity of another's strength.

4. *Trust is earned, not given. Not just others' trust in me, but my trust in them.*

5. *Treat others with the dignity and respect with which you desire others treat you.*

6. *Love yourself before all others.*

7. *Speak thoughtfully but openly. Don't worry about what others think; it's your life to live, not theirs.*

8. *Give back more than you take.*

9. *Walk upon the earth lightly, honor her as your first ancestor.*

10. *Value yourself and your services fairly, especially when compensation is involved.*

11. *Whatever you do, do it the best you can.*

KARMA

Watch your thoughts, for they become words.
Watch your words, for they become actions.
Watch your actions, for they become habits.
Watch your habits, for they become character.
Watch your character, for it becomes your destiny.[45]

There is a story about karma in which a powerful Witch was sitting in a meadow when a beautiful hummingbird began to sample the nectar of flowers nearby. The Witch admired the hummingbird and became lost in fascination until Death walked through the meadow. The Witch saw Death stop and look intently at the bird, then kept walking. Immediately the Witch knew that the hummingbird was in danger and drew upon her power and sent it far away to the west for safety. Satisfied, the Witch returned home. That night, the Witch dreamed of a hummingbird dead on the sands of the Western Sea. As they contemplated the dead bird, Death approached. The Witch asked, "Why did this hummingbird catch your eye?" and Death replied, "When I saw it, I knew it would die on the sands of a great sea, and I wondered how this tiny creature would end up in such a strange place to die."

---

45. Frank Outlaw, "Watch Your Thoughts," accessed September 29, 2020, https://quoteinvestigator.com/2013/01/10/watch-your-thoughts.

The word *karma* derives from the Sanskrit root *kri*, meaning "to do." Literally, "karma" means "doing," or "making" action. When used in a philosophical sense, it also has a technical meaning best translated as *consequence*, incorporating both an action and its consequence. Karma is a chain of causation that stretches back into the past and is therefore destined to stretch into the future's infinity. It is inescapable because it is universal, infinite, and, therefore, everywhere and timeless. Thus, the Witch of the story's karma is incurred in the act of carrying away the bird and its death in a strange place. The deed, pure in its content, led to an apparently unfavorable outcome. Is an action deemed positive or negative solely based on the result it generates or the intention behind the action?

Why worry over something we can't control? Things that seem adverse at the outset can end up helping us; something that seems attractive can hurt us. Good and evil are not constants; they change according to time and circumstance. An arrow is "good" if it pierces its objective; armor is "good" if it is impenetrable by an arrow.

We are accountable for what we are and what we wish to be; we make ourselves. If what we are in the present is the result of our past actions, it makes sense that what we wish to be in the future will result from our present actions. We have to know how to act. (And thus, karma ties into our ethics.)

Karma is like a huge boulder falling from the sky. Its falling does not deny you your free will; it's your decision about the falling boulder. Some will stand there waiting; others will try to run but are still crushed by the boulder. A Witch neither gives up nor runs away but acknowledges that the boulder is coming and does something about it.

Karma applies to the wrongs we commit, but also the virtuous actions we take. What goes around comes around—everything that we do will, in turn, be done to us; the good, the bad, and everything in between. Karma does not differentiate between good and evil; it only perceives action and reaction. Likewise, inaction is an action in this context.

Many people consider karma the consequences of our actions in previous lives, but reincarnation isn't part of the issue. Think about this: if you make a mess in the street, you may not ever be "punished" or "held accountable," but many people will start to avoid the street, some will worry less about making a mess there, the street will get dirtier, perhaps even to the point of being a danger to health, and so on.

Every action we take is an opportunity for growth, and we want to avoid looking at karma as merely a process of debts and repayment. When we make "right" decisions and actions, positive and rewarding opportunities tend to open their doors, even if we only recognize this in hindsight. Being responsible requires that we consciously make choices, knowing they will bring consequences, and accepting those outcomes as they manifest. Of course, we hope the consequences are positive.

Popular culture blames everything that goes wrong on "bad karma" in a confusion of bad karma with bad judgment. Not everything is the result of past actions. There may be a specific outline of life environs and circumstances resulting from the past, but we are developing new abilities and creativity within that outline.

Remember that living a positive and creative life in the present will resolve the past and set positive patterns for the future.

I suggest a simple answer: ask yourself one question each day: is there one who is glad that I have lived? If you can answer yes to this question, you are growing and evolving and have placed yourself on a positive spiral of spiritual evolution.

Disagreements often arise in our community about when it is and isn't appropriate to use magic—especially when other people are involved. Many say that you may not work magic unless you get the person's specific permission; it's an infringement on their will. A beautiful sentiment, but the truth is that we infringe on other people's will every single day: when we merge into traffic, apply for a job, buy the last plane ticket. If we concern ourselves with what other people want, we can lose sight of what needs doing.

It's a common practice to build in some kind of general statement in rituals designed to protect ourselves from creating *unintentional* harm.[46] Such phrases are handy but only work if you genuinely mean what you say; otherwise, they're just words, not intent or true will. The secret (if you can call it that) is that you must know yourself. Magic is not based on what you say, but instead, what you feel and the frame of mind you evoke. If you have good intentions, it does not

---

46. A concept I first learned from Marion Weinstein's excellent book, *Positive Magic* (New York: Earth Magic Productions, 1995) back when I was brand new to Witchcraft.

matter what you say or if you say the words at all, which is why meditation is so important—you need to have all your Selves aligned in intent.

Despite how it may sound, Witchcraft has no simplistic view of the universe with lords of karma acting as divine accountants of some kind who review every one of your actions, weigh it for good or ill, and tally up the balance before sending the appropriate punishment or reward. Instead, we believe that an intelligence takes our energy and reflects it as appropriate lessons for our betterment. Karma, therefore, is an active agent in our connection with the Universe.

THREEFOLD LAW

A lot of Witches think they *must* believe in the Threefold law, which goes something like:

Everything you do will come back to you three times over, including a (not very subtle) implicit warning to do only good, lest bad things come back to you. I don't know about you, but I left a religion that scolded me for making conscious choices (some of which aren't about doing "good") for another that instead allows me to take full responsibility for *all* of my choices. And that is a whole lot scarier than some nebulous universal force acting like a Cosmic Boomerang.

By taking personal responsibility, I am always saying, "the buck stops here." I have to ask for help when I need it, and I have to step up and own the consequences of my actions. There is no "just following orders" when *I* am the one giving the orders.

The Threefold law is an advisory effect on how we should honor ourselves and others by our words and deeds, not that we get back three times what we give out. If I give a dollar to a charity, it doesn't mean I'm going to receive three dollars back next week, next year, or whenever. It does mean that we receive value for value spent. For instance, if I give a hundred dollars to a friend in need but do not care if I get it back, I have invested threefold. Perhaps months later, I'm on a dark, windy road in a snowstorm, lost and worried because my car broke down and my phone has lost its charge. I trudge through the snow to a small service area that is closed. There is a payphone, but I have no change with me. A man walks out of the storm and approaches me; he is roughly dressed and has a sinister appearance. As he approaches, he smiles and hands me coins for the phone. I dial a number for assistance, and soon a friend is there to help me get home. Have I received three hundred dollars? No, but given by a stranger in a time of stressful need, that change is worth much more than the money I gave away. We have all been graced by the Threefold law at some time in our lives and likely didn't recognize its manifestation.

The trouble is that most of us have trouble shaking our religious upbringing, and that tends to be one in which if something terrible happens to you, you must deserve it. But when you extend it beyond your immediate situation, as most Pagans do, it takes on a different meaning. When bad things start happening in my life, I look at my surroundings and look for the potential lessons offered. I also check to see whether I've been conscious of my actions because I'm far from perfect and can make missteps.

I think right living is a matter of doing our best to take care of our body, eating as well as we can, getting some exercise, sleeping enough, laughing, crying when necessary, and loving whole-heartedly. Threefold, tenfold, a hundred-fold—the point is that the energy of our intentions and actions, like ripples in a pool, return to us amplified. What goes around comes around; recognizing the energies when they return is usually challenging because it won't reappear in precisely the same clothes it was wearing when it left the house.

HEXING AND HEALING

Some claim that a "real" Witch doesn't practice baneful Witchcraft, also called hexing. The word "hex" comes to us from the German *hexe*, which simply means "Witchcraft." In Pennsylvania Dutch country—made up of the present-day descendants of several waves of German-speaking immigrants from central Europe—*hex* refers to all sorts of folk magic, including the ubiquitous and beautiful signs that adorn their barns.

For me, Witchcraft includes hexing, cursing, binding, banishing, and other actions that change the larger reality in accordance with my will. I do not believe there is any risk of negative energetic feedback if the Work I do is in alignment. That is, my intention aligns with the required outcome, my correspondences are in order, and the forces petitioned to agree with the working. Hexing and healing are complex processes that require thought, perhaps divination, and the use of appropriate correspondences. Healing, even the sending of energy to another, can be incredibly toxic, especially if there is any denial about the disease. Healing menstrual cramps does nothing for the fibroids strangling the uterus. Protecting yourself from another through binding can be profoundly healing and powerful, yet it actively interferes with the free will of another. If that is holding you back from a binding, ask yourself why a stalker's free will has more importance than the person stalked. We use several lethal plants to treat ailments, such as belladonna for heart disease. Denying the full potential of the forces we work with is limiting, even disrespectful. How can we know the power of creation if we avoid destruction? Any gardener knows that we must clear the old growth before we can plant a new crop. It does no good to deny our ability to harm, deliberate or not. I know that I cannot become a better person if no one tells me how I act like a jerk—lots of people in my life can attest to my always saying "I can't fix it if I don't know about it." I think this sentiment is especially true of magic but not exclusive to it. It is likely to be far more apparent in magic because energy "coming home to roost" completing its circuit is what makes for effective magic in the first place. To my mind, it's a way of stating a universal law of physics, in which case it also requires a constant strive for improvement. We're human; we're going to make mistakes, that's normal. When we repeatedly make the same mistake, we begin to let ourselves and our practice down.

That is a difficult task, a lifetime's worth, or several.

Activity

Journal in your Book of Shadows about at least three times when the energy you sent out likely came back to you. I encourage you to avoid the trap of "good energy out = good things happened to me" and instead look for more complicated scenarios. Doing so can help you recognize potential scenarios in the future.

PRACTICE

Having established your foundation,
it's time to build the habits and
traditions that become
your spiritual practice.

PART 2

Chapter 6
IT'S ALL IN YOUR MIND

Here's your first lesson on the most critical skill a Witch can develop: mental focus. Without the discipline of controlled focus, absolute relaxation, and a quiet mind, your magical workings will simply not be as successful as they can be … if they succeed at all. These lessons need to be done daily for at least a month, as follows:

Week 1: Relaxation (you may add meditation after a few days)

Week 2: Start meditating, if you haven't already

Week 3: Add visualization

Week 4: Continue your meditation and visualization practices

Doing these exercises daily for a month will create a habit, a daily practice of mindfulness and stillness.

RELAXATION

It's a good idea always to do something relaxing
prior to making an important decision in your life.[47]

You may ask: Why learn to relax? For almost all of us, the stress of everyday living takes a physical toll on our bodies. We tense our muscles and our minds, often without being aware of it. Being able to relax:

+ is enjoyable.
+ helps you feel in control.
+ strengthens your belief in your ability to cope.
+ reduces the wear and tear on the body caused by chronic tension.[48]
+ reduces anxiety.
+ interrupts the stress cycle.
+ improves your quality of life.

When I first started as a Witch, I didn't think I needed to learn to relax; it seemed like I handled stress well and didn't notice any ill effects, all because my youthful energy was compensating for the toll that stress was taking on my body even then. So, I was sloppy and inconsistent about doing these techniques with any regularity. A very stressful several years of my life led to tension headaches and losing sleep. But when I returned to these relaxation techniques, I saw an immediate improvement in my health.

Preparing to Relax

When you are first learning these techniques, practice them in a quiet room, in a comfortable chair, and at a time when you are unlikely to be interrupted. For most people, this is either at the start of the day or as it winds down. Practice these techniques regularly, ideally twice a day; frequency is as important as the quantity of repetition when learning something new. It's a great idea to try mini-relaxations throughout your day. Try consciously relaxing whenever life pauses—at traffic lights, in the toilet, during commercials while watching TV,

---

47. Paulo Coelho, *The Pilgrimage* (New York: HarperCollins, 1987), 121.

48. Including: headaches, back and neck pain, fatigue, sleep disturbance, ulcers, lowered resistance to illness, and so on.

and so on. Different techniques work for different people, so here are a variety for you to try. If you find one isn't working after a few days of trying, move on to another.

Safe Space Relaxation

Because the mind and body are connected, a person can influence how their body feels through what their mind thinks. We have all had the experience of thinking of something frightening or sad, then physically experiencing that emotion. Likewise, when a person thinks of something relaxing and happy, there is a feeling of well-being and ease internally. As we think, so we become.

The following technique involves visualizing a special place that feels safe, relaxing, and happy. It's critical that you find a specific place and visualize the details clearly so that quickly recalling the place to mind is easy.

1. First, spend some time just settling deeper and deeper into the chair. Close your eyes. Breathe slowly and evenly, in and out.

2. Imagine yourself being in a special place, one where you feel completely relaxed and happy. Imagine you have been taken there by magic—to any place anywhere at all.

3. See yourself clearly in your mind enjoying this place. Clearly visualize the details. Who is there? What is happening? Become aware of the surroundings, the colors, the sounds, and smells. Allow yourself to feel utterly safe, relaxed, and happy. Enjoy these feelings. Allow them to flood through your whole body.

4. When you finish, allow yourself some time to reconnect before opening your eyes.

Deep Muscle Relaxation

This form of relaxation is a process of tensing and then relaxing different muscle groups. In this way, you will learn how to reduce unwanted tension in each one.

First, spend some time just settling deeper into the chair. Close your eyes. Breathe slowly and evenly, in and out, imagining the tension leaving your body, like a bird gliding away.

Tense each of the following muscle groups in the ways described below for about ten seconds. Let go of the muscle suddenly. Then give yourself 15 to

20 seconds to relax, noticing how the muscle group feels when relaxed in contrast to how it felt when tensed, before going on to the next group of muscles. You can also say to yourself, "I am relaxing," "Letting go," "Let the tension flow away."

Throughout the exercise, maintain focus on your muscles. When your attention wanders, bring it back to the pertinent muscle group.

Suggestions for Tensing Muscles

All these exercises are described as if you are standing. Please modify appropriately if you are instead sitting or lying down.

Lower arm: Make a fist, palm down, and pull your wrist toward upper arm.

Upper arm: Tense biceps, with your arm by your side, pull upper arm toward your side without touching. (Try not to tense the lower arm doing this, let that part hang loosely).

Lower leg and foot: Point toes upward to your knees.

Thighs: Push your feet hard against the floor.

Abdomen: Pull in your stomach toward your back.

Chest and breathing: Take a deep breath and hold it for about 10 seconds, then release.

Shoulders and lower neck: Shrug your shoulders, bring your shoulders up until they almost touch your ears.

Back of neck: Put your head back and press against the back of the chair.

Lips: Press your lips together, don't clench your teeth or jaw.

Eyes: Close your eyes tightly, but not overly hard.

Lower forehead: Pull your eyebrows down (try to get them to meet).

Upper forehead: Raise your eyebrows and wrinkle your forehead.

The entire practice session should take about 20 minutes. There's no need to rush through it; you are learning how your body feels when tense. If you don't have this much time, do fewer muscle groups rather than going through all of them faster. You'll likely have a sensation of momentum, which will be counterproductive to the feeling of relaxation you're aiming to create. You may feel very tired or drained. When you finish the last muscle group, give yourself time to reconnect with the world slowly, and gently open your eyes.

Breathing

Breathing changes when you are stressed; it becomes faster and higher in the chest. Most of us are aware of the relaxing feeling that accompanies a sigh. When we deliberately breathe deeper and slower, we tend to reduce the other signs of stress. When we engage in deep breathing, we stimulate the vagus nerve, the nerve that runs from the neck to the abdomen and is in charge of activating the "flight or fight" reflex.[49] If you're feeling anxious, try taking time to breathe deeply from the belly, at least once a day.

Creating a breathing practice allows us to be consciously aware and sense/feel/hear through our bodies. When we stop breathing easily, our bodies tense, our senses dull, and the mind gets frantic. In a sense, we lose consciousness. All alerts turn on, and the focus centers solely on feeding the brain. Most people walk around in just that state: apart and separate without even knowing why, just sensing something lacking. When we breathe consciously, we "attune" our senses in a clarifying, healthful, and inspirational way.

Here is a technique for learning to breathe consciously:

1. Place one hand on your abdomen right beneath your ribcage.
2. Take a slow, deep breath; feel your stomach rise as the breath moves down to your lungs.
3. Pause for a moment.
4. Slowly release the breath, making a quiet sigh and allowing your shoulders to drop as you exhale completely.

---

49. For more recent research on this nerve and how intertwined it is with the mind-body connection, see Edith Zimmerman, "I Now Suspect the Vagus Nerve Is the Key to Well-being," *The Cut*. Accessed December 31, 2019, https://www.thecut.com/2019/05/i-now-suspect-the-vagus-nerve-is-the-key-to-well-being.html.

5. Pause briefly and then repeat until you have completed ten slow, full abdominal breaths. Try to keep your breathing smooth and regular, without gulping in a big breath or letting your breath out all at once.

There are several breathing techniques out there, and you may find a different one is best for you.

When you first begin to breathe consciously, wear loose clothing and make sure your nostrils are clear. If you have a cold, allergies, or even a sore throat, wait until it's cleared before you begin; you will need to use your nose and a clear throat in this exercise. More than anything, don't get discouraged. It took me a while to get it down pat, feeling a bit clumsy. After all, it's only breathing!

MEDITATION

Let go of the past, let go of the future,
let go of the present, and cross over to the farther shore of existence.
With mind wholly liberated,
you shall come no more to birth and death.[50]

If you are anything like the typical person in the modern world, there is one thing you must do to improve yourself: you have got to reduce your stress level. While relaxation techniques have always been a part of a Witch's training, they have become critical in recent years. The level of stress in our lives has become a permanent state of emergency. Look, I know you have plenty of things to do. But most of us end up overeating, playing too many games, drinking too much, and doing everything but being intentional and conscious. I have a solution: meditate every day for at least twenty minutes.[51]

Meditation does not need to be complicated. Just sit comfortably and pick something you can focus on; your breath, a candle, some soft repetitive music,

---

50. Buddha, *The Teaching of Buddha: The Buddhist Bible: A Compendium of Many Scriptures Translated from the Japanese*, The Federation of All Young Buddhist Associations of Japan, 1934, 167, verse 348. Referenced at Bodhipaksa. Accessed October 18, 2020, https://fakebuddhaquotes.com/do-not-dwell-in-the-past-do-not-dream-of-the-future.

51. My Muay Thai instructor used to tell me: "Meditate for twenty minutes a day, unless you're busy. Then, meditate for forty minutes." Which sounds like a contradiction, but the point is that when you are feeling so stressed that twenty minutes feels like an imposition, it is more imperative than ever that you take measures to regain balance.

or sounds from nature. Every single time you catch your mind wandering, thinking or worrying about things, all you do is gently pull your attention back to your point of focus. Think about your brain as if it is a puppy. When we got our twelve-week-old dog Sasha, she was adorable and just wanted to play, explore, and get into things. We learned quickly that our job was to give her structure and bring her back to where it was safe for her to be. (Safe for her, safe for our furniture, safe for our floors. If you've ever had a puppy, you know what I mean.) I say this even though pretty much no one other than monks and nuns can stop their minds from bouncing around during meditation.

I've had a lot of students over the years who say, "I can't meditate; I just can't focus." I sympathize, but that's like saying, "I can't exercise; I get out of breath." We all know darn well that if we exercise regularly, we start out struggling but eventually we feel winded less easily. In the same way, you'll be better able to focus if you meditate consistently. The point is to do it daily, give it your attention, and be consistent. Many people view meditation as too complicated to learn, but many have engaged in it without realizing it. Have you ever watched a bird in flight or found yourself watching the water flow by in a stream or river? Maybe you listened to a favorite song and simply enjoyed the pleasure of it without following each line or word in detail. If the rest of the world around you seemed removed at that moment, you were meditating. Not so difficult, is it? Perhaps even enjoyable? For me, meditation is a way of grounding myself, reaching a place of peace and stability where I can find how I fit into the universe.

Another thing my students have told me is that trying to be still for twenty minutes stresses them out because it feels like a waste of time. Let me answer with a bit of factual data: the latest research shows that meditating for twenty minutes a day reduces the inflammation caused by stress, decreases blood pressure, enhances the ability to sleep, reduces chronic pain, and improves overall emotional health in every way.[52] Pretty good for twenty minutes a day, isn't it? On top of that, research also shows that people who meditate have a high level

---

52. "Meditation: In Depth," National Center for Complementary and Integrative Health. Accessed October 18, 2020, https://www. nccih.nih.gov/health/meditation/overview.htm. "Meditation: A simple, fast way to reduce stress," Mayo Clinic. Accessed January 22, 2020, https://www.mayoclinic.org/tests-procedures/meditation/in-depth/meditation/art-20045858.

of self-compassion, which allows them to succeed in long-term goals. Meditation is where you can catch negative self-talk and blow it away.

Witches meditate to tone the mind and get it into shape for ritual and magic. Most people aren't aware of the amount of noise their mind generates; this noise acts as static, interrupting the energy flows manipulated during ritual. Meditation eliminates (or at least reduces) the amount of static in one's mind. This sense of quiet within the mind acts as a kind of signal to the universe that we are in balance, both inner and outer realities act in harmony as we realize the relationships between the two states. Meditation becomes a bridge between the busy-busy-busy of the mundane world and the centered stillness of the sacred.

There are essentially four ways to meditate:

1. Sit still and empty the mind, letting any intrusion go, paying no attention to it.
2. Sit still and focus on a single image or word, letting any other intrusion go, paying no attention to it.
3. Move your body to music, paying attention only to your movements as you perform them with your mind otherwise empty.
4. Walking meditation (could also be running meditation).

That said, at this moment, there are 7.7 billion ways to meditate, one for each person on Earth (Note: please adjust your figures accordingly—the number has just gone up).

For each of the four ways described above are two main techniques, concentration meditation (focusing) and insight meditation (mindfulness). Most kinds of meditation use concentration. We focus our attention on a physical object such as a candle flame, sensation (whatever is felt while walking or breathing), emotion (such as reverence), mantra (spoken aloud or silently), or visualization (a flower in the mind's eye). Concentration meditation is a form of self-hypnosis.

Insight meditation is the analysis of thoughts and feelings in such a way as to cause realization of the subjectivity and illusion of experience. Such statements as, "this body is not me" fall under this category. We do this to attain transcendental awareness.

If you're worried about doing this practice "right," let me stop you there—there is no right. As long as you are reflecting or contemplating, you are meditating. Meditating on quiet and stillness is what most of us are thinking of when we talk about meditation, and it scares a lot of us and seems like something we couldn't possibly do. The point of meditation is not to silence our thoughts but to let them pass by. Accept at the outset that there will not be silence in your head for the entirety of your meditation session. It's all about flow: thought flows in, we observe it, and then allow thoughts to flow out. If even that sounds beyond you right now, be at ease. Even sitting with your thoughts while they are roiling is beneficial if you learn to observe those thoughts. That can be a valuable step on the path.

At its core, meditation is a kind of relaxed concentration to direct toward anything you wish: simple actions (chores), eating (savoring every bite and drink), a deity (visualizing your favorite god), a goal (an affirmation), or nothing at all. Meditation is best when incorporated into your daily activities by paying attention at all times. Keep track of where your feet are, where your hands are. Notice the flavor and texture of the food. Concentrate fully on whatever you're doing, wherever you are. As absurdly simple as that might sound, an untrained practitioner trying to observe *everything* they are doing will quickly wear out.

The techniques may vary between schools, but the basic concepts remain the same: to focus on one thought and selectively block out all others. The real key to this practice is exercising discipline over your thoughts and awareness of the world around you.

You may experience your external environment differently from usual as you continue your meditation practice. Colors, smells, and sounds may all seem amplified. We call this being in a trance state. People who achieve very deep trance states often report leaving their bodies—a phenomenon known as astral projection—or otherwise have psychic experiences. As you begin to meditate, the goal is not to get to a deep level—you are learning. If you do wish to enter deep states of meditation, I strongly recommend that you do so under the guidance of someone well trained in the practice of such techniques.

Set the stage for your meditation practice. Pick a place as private and safe as possible. You'll be entering an altered state of mind and deliberately turning your attention away from the outside world. I don't advise trying to meditate in a public place if there is a chance of being hurt. If you are at home and other are people present, make sure that you are not disturbed and that any noise in the house is minimized. You might hear from others that you ought to be able to meditate in the middle of a crowded city street and, sure, it is possible with practice, but why do that to yourself? There are a thousand metaphors, but basically: don't start learning something by doing the most demanding version of it.

When you start, you don't want to be too tired or have eaten a meal; you might fall asleep. That said, if you *do* fall asleep when you are learning to meditate, no harm done! You'll awaken refreshed and rested. But if you regularly fall asleep instead of meditating, look at changing some aspect of your practice, or get more sleep.

If you are lying down, be sure your back and neck are properly supported and don't fatigue your body. If you are sitting, be sure that both feet are flat on the floor and that you are sitting as erect as possible without being too stiff or strained. You should have your arms resting comfortably in your lap with palms up. It's essential that your body not become strained or fatigued for at least thirty minutes.

Begin with a visualization of protection.

Visualize yourself in a cocoon of white light that completely surrounds you. See the light as bright and warm. Say to yourself, "I am protected by the pure light of all that is good and truthful. I am surrounded by the pure light which keeps out all unwanted and evil influences."

This visualization is an excellent beginning. Some believe that we generate an aura that protects us from outside influences, not just when we are in a trance. Even if you do not accept this idea, the practice lends a feeling of safety and security. Nothing which is outside of you may enter or touch you without your permission.

The next step is learning to control and pay attention to your breathing. As a bonus, this breathing technique can relax and refresh you at any time and does not require the light sphere visualization.

Start by taking a deep breath in through your nose. Hold it for the mental count of 4, and then let it all out slowly through your mouth. Repeat this until you feel at rest, relaxed. Allow your breathing to settle into a steady, rhythmic rate.

Now see yourself lying in the warm light of the sun. The light is warm and pleasant. Starting with the tips of your toes, feel the light warming all of your body, slowly moving up into your legs, your trunk, and then into your arms and fingers. As you feel this warming, let yourself relax further, going deeper and deeper into a calm and quiet place.

When you feel completely relaxed and at peace, bring a single thought into your mind. It should be a pleasant experience or an idea such as love, joy, peace, or compassion. Focus on this one thought. If another thought tries to intrude, picture it as being written on a clear board between you and your focal thought. Then picture it being erased easily from that board. Deal with any thought other than your focal thought quickly. Try to maintain concentration on your focal thought for at least five minutes. Picture it as being genuine and experience it as if it were.

When you can do this and exclude all other thoughts as they attempt to enter your mind, you will have learned the single most important technique of meditation. It is now time to begin coming back to ordinary consciousness.

Slowly let the thought fade from your mind and again become aware of the warm light of the sun. As you feel the light bathing you in its warmth, start to reconnect your mind with the physical sensations of your body. Become aware of your breathing and the room around you. Do this slowly and calmly. When you are fully aware of your surroundings, open your eyes slowly. Enjoy the sense of calm and peace.

If you succeeded in doing this exercise, you should feel more relaxed and calmer than usual. It is important to remember to compare it to normal for *you*, not to what you think others would or should feel. If you do not feel you succeeded, try again in a day or two. Remember that the experience of meditation is a continuum, not a binary pass/fail state. It's just as true that five minutes is a checkpoint on your path, not the first "real" time, so don't dwell on "success" too strongly. Between meditation sessions, practice your deep breathing exercises. If you keep trying, you will soon reach a calm and meditative state. Do not attempt to meditate when you are ill, tired, or hungry. Those feelings only serve to make efforts more difficult. You cannot force yourself into a meditative state; you must flow into it and surrender to it calmly.[53]

Alternate Meditation Techniques

The most important attitude to take is that meditation isn't some exalted state of being which you can only achieve as a master. In its most elemental form, meditation is relaxation. Here are some examples of atypical meditative experiences:

+ **Consider your favorite place** or somewhere you'd like to be that has a lot to interest you and would keep your mind busy. Take yourself to that place. Imagine all the things you would see and respond to them just as if it were real life, meet people and create scenarios.

+ **Choose one image and focus on that.** Find an image that interests you, keep your "sight" on that, and nothing else. This technique is more for the visual person, but you can do the same thing with music or tactile manipulation, such as petting an animal. (My cat very much enjoyed this form of meditation!) You could use a mellow instrumental piece and focus on each note, going from one to the next. Remember that if you can stand it, monotony is like instant meditation. (If you have ever counted sheep to get to sleep, you know what I mean.)

+ Another method of meditation is to choose a calm, unvarying experience to visualize. For example, a long, winding river on a warm summer day is serene and continual. Imagine drifting freely like a leaf down the river. It is relaxing and unchanging. Imagine how it would feel to float upon it and nothing else. You could also imagine driving down a long-deserted road, coasting down an unending slope on a sled, or walking down the path in a forest with plain, simple scenery (just trees, trees, and more trees). Like the previous meditation, the repetitive, unchanging loop is what makes this work. Just make sure to choose an "activity" you are familiar with, enjoy, and understand.

---

53. Bill Witt, "Basic Meditation Techniques," *New Atlantic* BBS, May 1987, personal files.

+ Walking or other rhythmic movements can be meditation, especially if you find it difficult to meditate while seated or lying down. Take long, steady strides; focus on the feeling of the ground beneath your feet. Be in the present; notice what's around you. Walking meditation is especially helpful when you are feeling upset or have some problem to contemplate. I have had some of my most meditative experiences while swimming. I focus on the activity of moving my body, the sensation of the water, the relaxing feeling of stretching my limbs. If I am swimming a certain number of laps, I count them, often repeating the particular number I'm at over and over again. When I've finished swimming, I feel as if I've washed many of my worries and repetitive thoughts away from me; I feel clean, physically, mentally, and emotionally. Whenever doing this form of meditation, do it in safe, "calm" environments. There are many benefits to hiking a rugged trail, for example, but you've got to pay attention to what you're doing, so drifting off is inadvisable; zoning out while swimming in the ocean can be deadly.

How to Succeed at Meditation

All of my students struggle with meditation at first, but there are several extra things that will help you succeed. Remember that there is no right or wrong; there is only do.

+ Set a timer. You don't want to break your concentration by checking the time, so set a gentle (quiet) alarm to let you know when to return.
+ Avoid meditating on a full stomach, when overly tired, or while wearing restrictive clothing. Don't meditate while under the influence of alcohol or drugs. Some medications can interfere with the ability to be calm and focused. Use your best judgment.
+ It can be helpful to choose a hand posture (also called a *mudra*) to maintain while you are meditating. Mudras are another way to create physical triggers that prompt the brain to get into a meditative state, even if you aren't in your quiet place. Standard options are: touch your index finger and thumb, forming a circle, turn your hands so that your palms are facing downward, and then place them on your legs (*chin mudra*); you can make the same finger connection but turn

your hands, so your palms are facing up (*jnana mudra*); place the back of your right hand on the palm of your left hand, hands facing up and lightly resting in your lap (*dhyana mudra*).

VISUALIZATION

To bring anything into your life, imagine that it's already there.[54]

Visualization—the ability to see, hear, feel, touch, and taste with the inner senses—may be the most critical lesson in this module. Ultimately, you can't make magic happen without being able to see the outcome you desire. It is through internal images and sensations that we communicate with the younger self and the deep self. When the inner senses are fully awake, we may see visions of extraordinary beauty, smell the apple blossoms on trees, taste ambrosia, and hear the songs of Deity.

We know that our physical eyes do not actually "see" what is around them; they transmit light reflected from the objects we look at through the cornea onto the retina. The retina turns that light into signals that the brain can understand. It is the brain that sees, and it can see inner images as clearly as those in the outer world; in dreams, all five senses are vividly experienced and are no less tangible for not being physical. Put another way, all thoughts within your mind exist equally, whether you are considering an 'actual' object in front of you or are visualizing it completely via your imagination.

Some people naturally see images; others may hear or feel impressions. A few people find visualization difficult, but most find that the ability improves with practice. In fact, most people can develop the ability to use the inner senses vividly while awake.

One visualization exercise that many of my students find helpful (especially those with less experience in stretching their imagination) is to take an object—something simple but interesting—and focus on it quietly. A candle works great because you can turn out all the lights to block out other visual distractions that may surround you. Again, don't force anything; just observe at first. Then close your eyes and visualize the candle in your imagination. After

---

54. Richard Bach, *Illusions: The Adventures of a Reluctant Messiah* (New York: Dell Publishing, 2012), 114.

you get a good sense of the object, open your eyes, and check it. Start with short intervals, say five minutes, and then increase the time slowly.

Once you've mastered a simple object, repeat the exercise with another object. Then try it with two or more simple objects together. Always pick objects which hold your interest. As you grow more comfortable with the practice, you might consider moving on to symbolic items such as the Tree of Life diagram or tarot cards. For visualization of symbols used during ritual work, such as pentagrams, hexagrams, or circles, try drawing the symbols on a large white card using a vibrant color that catches your eye and matches the color you are going for in your ritual. Use the visualization technique above with the card, and soon you'll be able to visualize the symbol blazing in the desired color with hardly any effort.

Visualizing When You Can't

If you are not a visual thinker, you may wonder whether you can do magic at all—I want to reassure you that you can. I know many excellent practitioners who tell me they very seldom, if at all, "see" things on their journeys. Instead, they sense them. They have a sense of knowing what is there, where they are, what they are doing. Some report seeing colors or atmospheric shapes and textures but nothing distinct, yet they "know" that they are with other spiritual beings and allies within these sensations. Even though we tend to use vision-related language for the sake of convenience, your own experience of the sensations may be nonvisual.

Not being a visual person is different from the condition known as aphantasia, the inability to visualize images. First described in 1880, it has only recently become a focus of scientific study.[55] If you have aphantasia, visualization will need to involve constructing ideas and scenarios in your mind in ways that have nothing to do with images. Phrases you will need to transform in ways that make sense to you include:

+ Close your eyes, (description of scene)
+ Picture this:...
+ Imagine yourself in (described scene)

---

55. Anna Clemens, "When the Mind's Eye is Blind" *Scientific American*, accessed November 8, 2020, https://www.scientificamerican.com/article/when-the-minds-eye-is-blind1.

One alternative to seeing images is to create sounds to fill the scene being described or translate the scene into textures and tactile sensations. Another technique is to tell yourself a story. For example, if you're told to "imagine yourself on a beach," tell yourself a story of arriving at a favorite beach. Try to feel the sand under your feet, its heat and grittiness. Smell (or taste) the saltwater. Hear the seagulls and waves. Another technique is to focus purely on your emotional state. Instead of seeing the place, smelling the trees, and so on, feel the feelings that the idea of the place described brings to you. Continuing with the beach example, think of all the things you would feel if you were there: the beach is warm, comfortable, peaceful, relaxing, and so on.

Image Streaming Exercise

If you don't have aphantasia but struggle with visualizing, image streaming is another exercise to try.

+ Have an external focus, a friend, or a voice recorder.
+ Sit in a familiar place and look around. Close your eyes and describe what you see.
+ (Don't get frustrated!) Gently rub your closed eyes like a sleepy child. Then describe the bright sparkly light that you see behind your closed eyelid. Or look at a bright light like a candle for a half minute or a window with strong light/dark contrast. When you close your eyes, you should see afterimages, like a blob of light or color. Describe that blob of light.
+ Use all your senses—smell, taste, touch, sound, and sight—to describe the sparkly light or the blob.
+ While you are examining and describing your afterimages, be aware of any other kind of image. It could be a momentary glimpse of a face, landscape, or whatever. Notice when this happens, and try to describe that new image.

Practice image streaming for ten to twenty minutes a day to enable your mind's eye to see pictures.

Sensory Memory Exercises

If you don't have aphantasia but struggle with visualizing, this sensory memory exercise can work for you.

+ Choose a familiar place based on a distinctive sound. Describe that place in as much detail as you can. (For example, the sound of frogs on a spring evening.)

+ Choose a strongly tactile object. Describe it in as much detail as you can. (For example, your cat.)

+ Choose a wonderful aroma. Describe it and all the associations that it creates in your mind in as much detail as you can. (For example, freshly baked bread.)

+ Choose a delicious or distinctive flavor. Describe it and all the associations that it creates in your mind in as much detail as you can. (For example, the first time you ate a croissant.)

Practice sensory memory for ten to twenty minutes a day.

Problems You May Encounter

There are several common difficulties that people face when they begin to do mental work.

+ *Concentrating:* Nearly everyone has trouble keeping their mind on the task at hand. If you find your mind wandering, do not worry or get angry with yourself. Just notice that your mind has wandered, release the intruding thoughts, and deliberately turn your attention back to your focus. The more you practice, the less you will lose your focus.

+ *Feeling stressed:* On rare occasions, some people report nausea, dizziness, and feeling more stressed during and after relaxation. If this happens to you, it may be because the sensations you feel as your body starts to relax are unfamiliar to you. You may feel like you are losing control. Being aware of it might help. If not, try to relax with your eyes open or with a person you consider safe. Feel your way into being in your body when it is relaxed. If this is very difficult for you, therapy may be needed. Living in a body stressed to this point is unhealthy and damaging.

- *Giggling or feeling self-conscious:* Some people can't stop giggling or let go of the feeling of being self-conscious. Although this is more common in group situations, it usually eases the more you practice.
- *Falling asleep:* If you fall asleep, consider it a sign that you are overtired. Try to get more sleep at night and practice your mental exercises when you aren't tired, such as in the morning.

Activity

Keep recording your progress in your Book of Shadows. You are likely beginning to see how your outer behavior and inner reactions are changing due to your practice. You are not likely to see marked improvements immediately, but you *will* improve as long as you persevere.

Keep relaxing every day, especially if you have any stress in your life, but not as a part of your meditative and visualization practices. Instead, try the relaxation exercises before sleep or at the end of the day.

Meditate every day for at least a month. You can start right away by meditating or adding it in after a few days of just doing the relaxation exercises. Start with five minutes a day and see if you can work up to thirty minutes at a stretch. (If you already have a daily meditation practice, you don't need to change it.)

Visualize an apple. Hold it in your hands; turn it around; feel it. Feel the shape, the size, the weight, the texture, the temperature of the fruit. Notice the color, the reflection of light on its skin. Bring it up to your nose and smell it. Bite into it; taste it; hear the crunch as your teeth sink in. Eat the apple; feel it slide down your throat. See it grow smaller. When you have eaten it down to the core, let it disappear.

Taking your time, translate each of the following descriptions into a mental image. Sense (see, touch, hear, taste, smell) with your minds' eye:

- a familiar face
- a galloping horse
- a rosebud
- your bedroom
- a changing stoplight
- a newspaper headline

+ the sound of rain on the roof
+ the voice of a friend
+ children laughing at play
+ the feel of soft fur
+ an itch
+ a gentle breeze on your face
+ the muscular feeling of running and kicking a can
+ drawing a circle on paper
+ the taste of a lemon or toothpaste or a potato chip
+ the smell of bacon frying or a gardenia or perspiration
+ the feeling of hunger
+ a cough
+ coming awake
+ a stone dropped into a quiet pond with concentric ripples forming and expanding outward
+ these words flying away, high into the blue sky, finally disappearing
+ your shoe coming apart in slow motion and each piece drifting away into space
+ cutting an orange into five equal pieces, then arranging the pieces into equal patterns

Repeat this exercise in a few weeks and then a few weeks later. Notice any changes. Notice the difference in the way you see things—inner as well as outer—after you've done these exercises.

Bonus Material: Anchoring

You might add in the practice of anchoring as you train your mind to relax and eventually, to meditate. Anchoring is an effective way to train your body to relax by making an association in your brain between a state of relaxation and touching a specific spot on your hand or wrist quickly.

Choose a spot on your hand or wrist that will work as your anchor. (In the example following, we will use the fleshy part of your hand between the thumb and first finger called the purlicue as the anchor spot, but you can choose any spot that makes sense for you.) You will need to practice this technique several times to affix the anchor firmly. Generally speaking, after three sessions, you will notice that you relax when you squeeze your purlicue. Whatever spot you choose, consistently use this same location.

Anchoring Script

This script guides you to relax your body using progressive muscle relaxation, passive progressive relaxation, and stretching. Once you are relaxed, you will use anchoring to associate the relaxed state with a physical trigger so that you quickly achieve the state of relaxation without going through the entire relaxation process. (I chose this location when I started my practice because it felt natural. It turns out that this is a pressure point and that firmly holding it can relieve headaches.) I strongly recommend that you record this script rather than try to read and do it simultaneously. When you read the script, take your time. Go slower than typical. Consciously breathe slowly and deeply to find a relaxing rhythm. There is a natural pause built into this script every time you say the word "relax." You may need to re-record the script to find the right pace.

Now it is time to relax and begin the process of anchoring.

Begin by stretching out your muscles gently. Raise your arms above your head as you breathe in and lower your arms to your sides as you exhale. Repeat.

Roll your shoulders forward. and back. Now relax. Let the tension drain away from your shoulders.

Now that you have moved your shoulders and arms to allow your body to begin to release the tension it has been holding, find a comfortable and relaxed position sitting or lying down.

Stretch the muscles of your face as you open your mouth wide and breathe in. Yawn if you wish. Stretch the muscles of your face, and let your face slacken gently as you breathe out. Relax completely. Let your lower jaw hang loosely below your upper jaw, your teeth not touching.

Scan your body for areas of tension as you take in another deep breath. Feel the tension in your body as you hold that breath. Now let the tension go as you let the breath go.

Point your toes, stretch your legs. Release the muscles of your legs and relax. Now bring your feet upward toward your shins, stretching the back of your legs. Release the stretch, relaxing your legs completely.

Let your legs become limp, loose, and relaxed. Let your arms become relaxed and loose.

Notice how your body feels. Feel the relaxation flowing through your body. Notice that you can become even more relaxed. Wiggle your toes once or twice, and then allow your toes to be still and relaxed. Feel the relaxation flowing, spreading, until your feet are relaxed as well.

Let the relaxation continue to your ankles. Feel how loose and relaxed your ankles feel. Now allow the muscles of your lower legs to give up their hold. Feel the relaxation in your lower legs calm. Relaxed, heavy, relaxed.

Enjoy the feeling of relaxation as it continues to your knees, then your upper legs. Feel your thighs legs relaxing and letting go. Your legs feel very heavy, very heavy, and very relaxed.

Feel the relaxation flowing. Allow your buttocks to relax. your pelvic area. and now your abdomen. Feel the muscles becoming loose and relaxed, letting go of all the tension, relaxed and heavy.

Allow your lower back to relax. Feel the relaxation there as the muscles of your lower back give up their hold, leaving nothing but relaxation and calm.

Let the relaxation continue to flow throughout your body, spreading now to the muscles of your sides. feel your sides, abdomen, and chest gently moving in and out with each breath. Each breath makes you even more relaxed.

Allow the muscles of your sides to let go. Feel the relaxation filling your core. relaxing your chest and stomach, your middle back, your upper back.

The relaxation continues to increase. pleasantly more and more relaxed, deeper and deeper. Feel your shoulders relaxing, your upper arms, your elbows.

Feel your arms relaxing more and more. becoming heavier and heavier let the relaxation continue spreading to your lower arms, your wrists, and your hands. Your arms become entirely limp and relaxed. Pleasant. Relaxed.

Let the relaxation continue from your lower back, middle back, and upper back to your neck, the back of your neck, and the front of your neck. Now to the back of your head, the top of your head, your chin, your face, your jaws.

Feel your cheeks relaxing, becoming completely loose and relaxed. Feel your lips relaxing, becoming soft and relaxed. Let your tongue relax. Feel your nose relaxing, let your eyes relax. Your eyelids are very heavy and relaxed. Feel your eyebrows relaxing and your forehead becoming smooth, calm, and relaxed. Your whole body is now fully relaxed

Enjoy the relaxation you are experiencing and gently squeeze the purlicue of your left hand while at the same time silently saying "Relax," anchoring the feeling of relaxation to this motion.

Experience the feeling of deep relaxation. Notice your breathing. Notice how calm and regular your breathing is. Watch your breathing without trying to change it in any way.

As you breathe in, silently say "I am relaxed."

As you breathe out, silently say "I am calm."

I am relaxed.

I am calm.

I am relaxed.

I am calm.

Again, squeeze your purlicue while mentally saying, "relax." Let the anchoring occur as this spot becomes associated with your peaceful, relaxed state.

Feel the relaxation deepen each time you squeeze your right thumb while saying "relax." Continue to allow the relaxation to flow throughout your body. Calm. Peaceful. Relaxed.

Memorize this feeling of relaxation. Notice how your body feels. Notice how calm you are. Create a picture in your mind of this state of relaxation. With this image in mind, gently squeeze your purlicue one more time while saying to yourself, "relax." Feel the relaxation deepen.

This spot is an anchor to remind you of the relaxation you are feeling right now. In the future, anytime you squeeze your purlicue, the feelings and memories of how relaxed you are right now will fill your mind, and your body will automatically relax.

You are as relaxed as you want to be.

Calm.

Relaxed.

Warm. Safe. Comfortable. Relaxed

Now it is time to start to become aware of your surroundings and return to your usual level of alertness. Keep your eyes closed a few moments while your body reawakens.

You can use anchoring at any time to cue your body to relax. Remember the pleasant, peaceful state of relaxation, and know that your anchor can remind you of the relaxation you experienced.

Count up from one to five, becoming more alert with each number, until at five you are fully awake and alert.

One, becoming more awake, more alert, and energetic.

Two, feeling calm, awakening even more.

Three, almost totally awake now, ready to resume your day.

Four, eyes open, stretch the muscles, becoming completely awake.

Five, fully awake, fully alert, rested, and ready to go.

Chapter 7
ENERGY WORK

The soul is invisible. An angel is invisible. The wind is invisible. Thoughts
are invisible. And yet, with sensitivity, you can see the soul, you can guess
the angel, you can feel the wind. And you can change the world with only a
few thoughts.[56]

Witchcraft is a path of pleasure in and gratitude for the beauty of nature. Our
every act could reflect that pleasure, even those that are invisible. Almost all
our work involves energy, not just spell work, but also our worship, celebration,
and personal development. Many of us don't think about the energy we regularly use in our daily lives in mundane tasks; our energy is there when we need
it. For magic, it's not so simple. This lesson guides us in paying attention to our
energy and learning to manipulate and focus on what we wish. Keep in mind
that energy work is not always sequential, nor is it a task you do only once. You
will return to this lesson many times as you go forward with your practice.

---

56. Shared on Twitter by @paulocoelho, 7:38pm, Dec. 26, 2018.

DEFINING ENERGY

A friend once told me:

> I have always had problems with using the term 'energy' to describe
> magical effects. As an engineer by profession, "energy" has a very care-
> fully defined meaning in my engineering work. In magic, it is not so well
> defined. "Energy" seems to be a catch-all term with no proper meaning
> at all.[57]

It's a good point; after all, most of us think about energy as something
along the lines of Einstein's $E=mc^2$ equation. But magical energy has nothing
to do with mass. Many people in the alternative spirituality landscape seem to
have adopted the term "energy" to describe anything that produces the slightest
sensation, motion, or result. The term has taken quite a beating and become
nearly useless.

Witches access and manipulate energy within a symbolic framework to produce a specific effect. Doing so may include connecting the immanent Deity to
the external Deity.

Science has proven that our universe is made up of atoms, formed from
three tiny particles: protons, neutrons, and electrons. Protons carry a positive
electrical charge, electrons carry a negative electrical charge, and neutrons carry
no electrical charge. An atom fuels itself, like a perpetual motion machine,
and that energetic cycle is the fundamental building block of life. Think about
atoms as being like the charges on a car battery; electrons = negative = black,
and protons = positive = red. To power the car, you need both charges. Since
atoms all matter in our universe is formed from atoms, everything in our universe is made of energy; and our magic manipulates it. There are many forms
of energy, including within the visible spectrum, within sound, and the electromagnetic spectrum.

When we work energy, we rely upon our psychic abilities as effortlessly as
our ordinary senses. *Psyche*, the Greek word for soul, refers to things beyond
the known physical world, knowledge that comes from more than our five
senses. Psychic phenomena include intuition, sensing the unseen, and hearing

57. J∴M∴555, private discussion, January 2000.

voices. Although most of us will need to develop the ability, we are all psychic to a greater or lesser degree.

Psychic abilities, once developed, can become quite powerful. By engaging in this work, you are metaphorically stepping away from most others and asking the Universe to pay special attention to you. In doing so, you agree to be held accountable to its laws, the first of which is that *the energy you send out will come back to you.* This is very nearly common sense. In any given situation, your responses alter and affect the environment and how others react to you, even if it's not a clear and precise action/reaction effect. Generally speaking, if your response is highly emotional, the situation will become more intense; if your response is calmer, it will often shift the feeling to a more neutral scenario. It isn't always 1:1, nor do I mean to imply any form of victim-blaming. Bad things happen and aren't necessarily the fault of the person they happen to. Someone in a violent relationship didn't "call" that violence upon themselves. Whether financially, emotionally, or economically, someone in survival mode didn't "ask" for hardship. Someone with cancer isn't refusing to process their emotional/karmic/spiritual/whatever issues. As Witches, we recognize that we are responsible for our reactions, for the energy we put into situations. So the more neutral, reasoned, calm, and positive our energy output, the more that type of energy will exist in our environment.[58]

The second law of energy is the greater your awareness, the greater your responsibility. It is rarely acceptable to use your magic to manipulate or assume power over others. Note that I said "rarely"—we live in a world full of injustice, imbalance, and outright violence, which tends to create a mindset of fear. When we act from a place of fear, our core desires are for retaliation rather than reconciliation. Doing the work to change those desires takes time, so my caution for seekers is to work from a place of "harm none" until they are truly comfortable with their Craft and have a high level of self-knowledge. There are usually many options to pursue before using one's magic to hurt another. While I am a firm believer that while Witches heal, we also hex, using magic to cause harm or deliberately manipulate another. It is advanced-level work only to be done after a great deal of introspection.

---

58. Yet another reason for having a meditation practice. A calm mind allows for a higher chance of a calm reaction to external strife.

A good place to start is our personal energy, the energy that emanates within and from ourselves. This type of energy includes our metabolism, heat, and the invisible force that some martial arts practices call *chi* or *ki*. Our personal energy can be affected by ordinary means: positively by eating correctly, exercising regularly, and sleeping enough, or negatively via illness, overwork, or self-neglect. It can also be affected by emotions, psychological issues, and spiritual exertions. These forms of energy are interrelated in complicated ways that can be beneficial (such as when we stay up all night to meet a deadline) or harmful (such as "self-medicating" psychic wounds with drugs, food, or alcohol).

Energy is all around you; it cannot be created or destroyed, only transformed. You are being bombarded by energy all the time, often without realizing it: radio waves, light waves, sound waves. The forces of gravity pull down upon you constantly, and air continually presses against you. The energy in your body and the energy in the universe is the same. Sometimes the energy expands, and sometimes it contracts. Both patterns are necessary for life, as in breathing, both inhalation and exhalation are essential. Without that continual flow, there could be no motion, no action, and therefore no life. Universal energy is always available to you; you have all the energy you need. Each time you give out energy, new energy flows into its place. Most of us are aware of another person's energy. Often if we feel tense, tired, or relaxed in the company of another person, it's because we are absorbing or resonating with their energy. Once aware of your energy and the energy of others, you can begin to share that energy, raising more energy or getting in touch with universal energy for the formation of a circle. When we build and share energy in ritual, we call it raising a cone of power.

A few notes about the energy work in this lesson:

+ The following activities and exercises need to be done, not just read. You must actively participate in this to have any kind of benefit at all.

+ Don't expect any shortcuts. Many of these activities will eventually be very quick for you, or you'll be very familiar with them, and so they will not take as long. But in the beginning, doing these activities will take you longer if only because you're unfamiliar with them.

+ Read through every exercise entirely at least once before you try it. It can be beneficial for you to record your voice reading through the exercise beforehand.

+ These activities are examples, and there are many versions available in the world. If you don't succeed with the ones offered here, look for similar ones so that you can find what works for you.

+ Most of these exercises presume the modifier, "as well as you can do so." Try your best, and modify when you need to.

PREPARING FOR ENERGY WORK

Cleansing your energy and the physical space you work in will be folded into your grounding and centering process as you progress. For now, I'm going to call it out separately as we get started.

Space Cleansing

Space cleansing purifies an area in a sort of psychic removal of the dead or unwanted energies that naturally build up in our lives. Although you may want to make modifications for spaces you share with others, this practice works almost anywhere.

Begin by clearing and balancing your energy. Breathe deeply and allow all mundane concerns to float away. Standing in the area you intend to cleanse, set your intent by saying to yourself:

By my will I cleanse this space.
I banish all negativity from this place.

At the same time, imagine the area filling up with bright light into every nook and cranny. (Traditionally this color is white or gold, but it's best to use a color you find pleasing and associate with "clean.") As it does so, know that all negativity is fleeing from the light, leaving only clear space behind. If you have privacy, you can add clapping or smoke cleansing with incense or sage to intensify the effect.

Imagine the light turning to a color you associate with protection, filling the space with its shielding energy that prevents any negativity from returning. When finished, say:

I welcome peace and creativity.
As I will, so mote it be.

Activity
Journal about this cleansing in your Book of Shadows. How does your experience with this exercise change (or not) over time?

Grounding
Grounding is an essential skill for spiritual hygiene, providing you with both a source of clean, protective energy and an outlet for excess or unbalanced energy. Think of it as a kind of lightning rod that attracts and reroutes harmful or excess energy before it can harm you. Grounding is a core practice for doing magic. Without being grounded, you are likely to feel disconnected physically, emotionally drained, irritable, restless, or anxious after doing magical work. To ground, extend your energy body down into the earth and establish your connection in the physical plane on several levels. Grounding stabilizes you so that whatever happens around you, you remain focused. When we ground, we get rid of excess energy or replenish low levels. When we ground, we calm our emotions and soothe our nerves. Being grounded also means we are mindful of our environment.

When you are solidly grounded, you are more aware of your own body's sensations and energy patterns in addition to the world around you. Doing so helps you respond to the world more immediately and appropriately, helping you stay in the present moment, letting the past remain behind you while trusting that the future will bring great things. The saying goes, "If you are depressed, you are living in the past. If you are anxious, you are living in the future. If you are at peace, you are living in the moment"[59] to which I would add, "if you are at peace, you are grounded."

Grounding is a vital skill for healing, magic, and even more so for healthy living. When you start to feel stress, worry, anger, hopelessness, or any other emotion that erodes your peace, take a bit of time to ground. In doing so, you

---

59. Attributed to Lao Tzu, but more likely from Rev. Run in his 2006 book, *Words of Wisdom* (New York: HarperCollins), 31. Stefan Stenudd, "If you are depressed …" Fake Lao Tzu Quotes, accessed October 18, 2020, https://www.taoistic.com/fake-laotzu-quotes/fake-laotzu-quote-If_you_are_depressed_you_are_living_in_the_past.htm.

will shift your energy and start to feel calm and in control, allowing you to get greater clarity about your situation.

Ideally, we go through life in a grounded state: we experience life entirely and interact with everything and every being naturally. We know who we are and what we want; we can speak our truth and be authentic. We've got it together, and the vagaries of life are just things to deal with, not crises. When we are ungrounded, we are "off": off-kilter, overly emotional, unable to cope with life, out of control, spacey. Being ungrounded happens to most of us who work with energy at some time or another, and it can be extremely uncomfortable or even scary.

There are several ways to ground, some of which aren't healthy for long-term use. Anything that brings you back into your physical body is something that grounds you.

The most common method is to use visualization. Get as comfortable as you can (ideally sitting down), close your eyes, and imagine that you have roots like a tree, growing out of your feet (or buttocks) into the earth below you. (It does not matter if you are in a skyscraper or sitting on the ground). Visualize those roots reaching down to the center of the earth. As you root, feel the smooth, substantial, warm energy of the earth flow up the roots and into your body. Feel the slow warmth rise up your legs into your belly, your chest, across your shoulders, and into your head. Feel the heartbeat of the earth mirroring your heartbeat, syncing in time. Remain in this state of connection as long as you want or can. When you are ready, let the earth's energy flow back out of you, slowly releasing you and leaving you feeling refreshed and calm.

Another technique is to go out into nature: go for a walk, sit under a tree, lay down on a huge rock, watch a waterfall or the ocean waves.

The quickest method is perfect for after ritual or any energetic work. Place your hands flat on the ground (again, it doesn't matter if you are indoors or even on ground level) and feel your connection to the earth. Let any excess energy flow out of you. If you feel like your energy is low, go ahead and pull some up (slowly) to replenish and balance you.

Other grounding practices are to eat a meal or make love. Eat delicious, healthy food with complete attention and enjoyment. Delight in your lovers' body (or your own) as you sensuously explore and connect physically. Both will get you back into your body in a delightful way, especially if you bring your full consciousness and awareness to it. Other ways to ground include going to the toilet, petting animals, and gardening. Dancing and stomping your feet can be a fun way to ground, as is laughing with friends.

The not-so-healthy ways to ground probably won't come as a surprise: smoking, alcohol, coffee, (recreational) drugs, and chocolate. All will be enjoyable at the moment but making a habit of using them to ground or in any way affect your energy has longer-term negative consequences. The most straightforward example is coffee. So many of us have a cup (or three) in the morning to wake up and get going. Then it's hard to get to sleep at night, or we don't sleep well, and the coffee becomes necessary to get started. When you start adding in the necessary glass (or three) of wine to relax and wind down at night, you've created a nasty cycle.

If this sounds familiar to you, I encourage you to do your best to find other, more supportive ways of grounding. No guilt! Start doing visualizations or walks alongside your current habits. Make small changes, take small steps, change your habits, and celebrate the small success. Eventually, other things can fall away.

Rooting

Rooting is a basic grounding technique in which you visualize roots coming out of you and going into the Earth. Many people do this sitting, but you can also do it standing. I don't recommend doing it lying down—it's too easy to fall asleep!

Close your eyes and take three deep, slow breaths. Focus on the base of your spine if you're sitting, and imagine roots coming out from your spine and moving down into the earth. If you're standing, imagine those roots coming out from your feet and moving down deep into the earth. Push those roots deep into the ground, making their way easily and steadily down, deep into the core of the Earth. When you've gone far enough (and you'll know when that is), visualize your energy connecting with the Earth Energy and like a tree pulling that deep Slow Earth Energy up into your body and moving it throughout your body. You should feel calm, reconnected, and focused. When finished, visualize those roots slowly withdrawing from the earth and pulling back into your body again, leaving you calm and refreshed.

I recommend start by grounding at least two to four times a day. The minimum would be once in the morning and at bedtime; adding in lunchtime, and the late afternoon is excellent. When you practice grounding regularly, you will become able to stay grounded and balanced for more extended periods.

Centering

There's a center of quietness within, which has to be known and held.
If you lose that center, you are in tension and begin to fall apart.[60]

Centering is the process of finding our core and connecting our mental energy and focus with our spiritual essence. It's a matter of being in alignment so wholly that we know precisely what "me" and "not me" are. The phrase "pull yourself together" is appropriate here. Knowing the difference between "me" and everything else is necessary before starting anything that might contact other energies or places (such as scrying or astral projection). When we center ourselves, we align ourselves—higher, middle, and lower; physical, mental, emotional, and spiritual—with our intent and will. We create a strong connection of wholeness and integrity.

When you are centered, you are calm and aware of your intuitive thoughts and feelings. It is a dynamic process of psychic equilibrium. Although it doesn't have a location, you center by focusing your attention within your body.

There are many methods to center. A simple version is to close your eyes and concentrate on a point within the center of your body; deep in the pelvis, right around your belly button, or in the diaphragm, right below the center of your chest. Feel your pulse in your wrist or neck. Let your pulse soothe you for a time, then inhale for six beats, hold for three beats, exhale for six beats, hold for three beats, and repeat. It feels difficult at first, but within minutes your heart rate will slow and you will be able to lengthen the beat pattern to 4-8-4-8 and so on.

Centering is a natural part of grounding, usually done at the same time. The following exercise expands on the rooting method of grounding above and is one of my all-time favorites for grounding and centering.

---

60. Joseph Campbell and Bill Moyers, *The Power of Myth*, (New York: Anchor Books, 1991), 161–162.

Tree/Sky Visualization

Sit comfortably with your spine as erect as possible while remaining relaxed. (You may want to sit in a chair with a straight back or on a pillow with your legs crossed in front.) Place your hands on your knees.

Breathe deeply from the belly, relaxing with each breath, allowing any negativity to flow out of you with each exhalation. Release all mundanity and trivia. When you are completely clear, go to the next step.

Continue breathing deeply and feel your spine get just a little bit straighter. Feel energy rising within you as you do so. Imagine that your spine is the trunk of a tree. From the base of your spine, small roots extend deep into the earth. They move deeper into the earth and begin to draw upon her energy. This energy begins to climb your spine, like sap rising through a tree trunk. Feel the power rise your spine with each breath. Feel yourself becoming more alive with each breath.

Once the energy reaches your head, feel the energy reaching outward, like branches. Feel those branches extend up and into the air, connecting with the sky above.

You are now connected to the earth and the sky, their power flowing through you up and down, down and up, an endless flow through your body. Relax and feel the power moving through you.

Take a deep breath and feel the branches pulling back into you, release the sky. Feel the power flow down into the earth as your roots retract. You are yourself once again.

Relax.

Activity

Journal about the experience of grounding and then centering in your Book of Shadows. How does your experience with this exercise change (or not) over time?

MANIPULATING ENERGY

Manipulating energy is the core of working magic. Knowing your energetic pattern is the first step in manipulating other energy patterns, so we start there. To feel your energy, here are several exercises. When doing these exercises at the outset, you might not feel anything or dismiss what you feel as it is so subtle that it must not be real. You may feel a sense of force or pressure, kind of like playing with two magnets, feeling them attract and repel one other depending on how you turn them. You might feel a slight temperature shift, typically a sense of warmth. You might feel a slight tingle or a pins-and-needles kind of a sensation or (more rarely) a kind of numbness.

Generally speaking, working with energy, is a tactile sensation. Still, it is also possible to work with energy and experience it through one of your other senses in a primary way. Always be open to whatever sensations you are experiencing and accept that as your truth. As you do these practices, don't hurry. Allow the spirit of play to inhabit you and pay attention throughout.

Sensing

Make yourself comfortable. Clear your head and body of any negativity, let all your worries and mundane concerns drop away. Breathe deeply and calmly, allowing the air to fill you and drive away any negativity. Continue to breathe deeply and evenly throughout this exercise.

For about 10 seconds, rub the palms of your hands together in a swift, circular or back-and-forth motion. (Your palms will likely feel warm.) Move your hands apart 12 to 18 inches and notice the "tingling" feeling emanating from your palms. Slowly move your palms together until you feel a sense of resistance or an increase in heat. It can be warm, hot, cool, or cold. It can be heavy or light. It may even be a tingling sensation. Each person experiences energy differently.

Ball of Light

Once you can sense the energy, you can start to play with it. Place the palms of your hands together. Feel your palms grow warm where they touch, and imagine that heat is light. Imagine it clearly and powerfully. (If just putting your hands together doesn't generate the sense of energy, go back to the sensing exercise to generate the energy, then continue with this exercise.)

Slowly pull your hands apart and feel that light turn into a ball of light between your palms, not quite touching you, but hovering between your hands. How big can you make the ball? How small? Does it change in intensity or warmth as you change the size?

Open and close both hands rapidly 10 or 20 times, then reverse the palm up/palm down positions and repeat the hand openings.

Bring your hands together and allow the light to dissipate. Allow any excess energy to run through you, through the soles of your feet into the earth. Another way to dissipate the energy is by clapping the hands sharply together. That disrupts the energy pattern while still keeping it in your aura. You should feel calmly energized.

Journal about the experience in your Book of Shadows. How has your experience changed (or not) over time?

Different Shapes

Make yourself comfortable. Clear your head and body of any negativity, let all of your worries and mundane concerns drop away. Breathe deeply and calmly, allowing the air to fill you entirely and drive away any negativity. Continue to breathe deeply and evenly.

Place the palms of your hands together. Feel your palms grow warm where they touch, and imagine the heat is, instead, light. Imagine it clearly and firmly. Pay attention to the energy. Does it pulse?

Slowly pull your hands apart and feel that light turn into a ball of light between your palms, not quite touching you but hovering between your palms. Notice how the energy changes (or doesn't).

Change the shape of the ball to a beam, a bar, or any other shape that feels appropriate. Does the energy change when you do so?

Bring your hands together and allow the light to dissipate. Allow any excess energy to run through you, out the soles of your feet, into the earth. You should feel calmly energized.

Journal about the experience in your Book of Shadows. How has your experience changed (or not) over time?

Playing with Colors

Make yourself comfortable. Clear your head and body of any negativity, let all of your worries and mundane concerns drop away. Breathe deeply and calmly, allowing the air to fill you entirely and drive away any negativity. Continue to breathe deeply and evenly throughout this exercise.

Place the palms of your hands together. Feel your palms grow warm where they touch, and imagine that heat is light. Imagine it clearly.

Slowly pull your hands apart and feel that light turn into a ball of colored light between your palms, not quite touching you, but hovering between your palms. How many colors can you visualize? (Start with sequential colors: yellow, orange, red, green, blue, purple, white.) Can you make a rainbow of several (or all seven) colors appear? Do the colors affect the light's strength or intensity?

Bring your hands together and allow the light to dissipate. Allow any excess energy to run through you, through the soles of your feet into the earth. You should feel calmly energized.

Playing with energy gets you used to it, so have fun. Journal about the experience in your Book of Shadows. How has your experience changed (or not) over time?

Activity

Actively apply the principles you read about to your daily life: pay attention to when you feel grounded and ungrounded throughout the day. See if you can sense energy and its fluctuations around you as well as within you. Does your environment change as your energy changes?

Once you are comfortable with all of these exercises, take the energy ball and press it into a crystal, rock, or candle with a locking phrase, such as "So Mote It Be," "Amen," or "Blessed Be." The phrase helps you key into the fact you want this energy to stay where you put it. This is known as charging an object. After you've charged an object, feel it, and see if you can find where the energy field begins. Can you tell when the charge begins to wear off?

Once you can charge objects, practice stripping them of energy or using the energy in deliberate ways. Once you are comfortable with this practice, you can cleanse magical objects by pulling the energy out of them and then grounding the energy into the earth.

In your Book of Shadows, write your observations from these activities and the results of your efforts.

RAISING ENERGY

Raising energy is the peak of your ritual, the focus of your spell. It is also the most difficult to describe as it is entirely experiential. We start from the premise that everything in life has energy. It binds us, connects us, and works with or against us. Think of the last concert you went to when the music utterly enthralled the crowd. There you all were, wiggling and dancing, bopping around, caught up in the rhythm and power of the performers. That feeling, that energy, is what you want to create in your rituals. The performer was able to engage you completely and you were able to lose yourself in it.

For most people, one of the core tenets of Witchcraft is to do magic. Doing so requires combining your will with your intention and using energy to direct and manifest your will into reality. Directing energy requires creating an altered consciousness through either meditative practice or ritual. Working magic requires a focused will to direct energy raised towards a specific purpose. Typically, you raise and work energy through altering your consciousness but there are more straightforward ways to practice using energy. No situation is too trivial or too big; you can alter the energy of the universe.

When working with others, our energies are shared, even in non-magickal contexts, like an office. But when we work with others magickally and form close, intimate spiritual relationships, our shared energy creates a kind of pool we call an egregore. Any member of the group can tap into the egregore and it, along with a shared heritage of techniques, forms a rich gift that cannot be duplicated by the solitary Witch.

In a group, the raising of energy is often described as creating a cone of power and it's creation is at the direction of a specific person, allowing everyone to focus their energy with the effort coordinated. The cone shape illustrates how the energy raised stays within the circle and builds to a peak, after which it is sent toward the ritual or spell's purpose, shooting out of the topmost point, like an arrow made of pure power. When working alone, you are automatically the one leading and directing the energy. When doing your ritual or spell, raise the energy until it feels exactly right, and then send it on to do your will. Learning to know when "exactly right" is will take practice and will change if you add or change people.

Techniques for Raising Energy

There are eight primary ways to raise energy. Some techniques work better than others in different settings. For example, your neighbors might object to you turning the music up loud or dancing over their heads. Different ritual purposes (yoga to heal a broken leg is an odd choice) and the number of participants (silent meditation is most comfortable when solitary, binding is nearly impossible—and not safe—when alone) will call for different methods. There are three techniques I either do not recommend or include here with great caution for newcomers. The eight techniques are listed below based on how easy it is for newcomers.

1. Singing and Dancing

The concert analogy above is great because singing and dancing are the easiest ways to raise energy for most people. I have a collection of music guaranteed to get me moving, and I love to use it for ritual. There are fewer songs I sing in ritual, but the power of the classic sustained "OM" will shift me into an altered state quickly, as will a couple of "traditional" Pagan chants.[61] Here are a couple of my favorites:

Isis, Astarte, Diana
Hecate, Demeter, Kali
Inanna[62]

———

She changes everything she touches.
Everything She touches changes.

Singing to raise energy requires privacy so that you won't be disturbed. Start by breathing deeply, centering yourself, and bringing yourself to the present moment. Focus on your goal/intention/desire. Begin chanting in a low voice, calmly and quietly. As you repeat your chant, increase the force and loudness

---

61. The work of Laboratorium Pieśni/Song Laboratory is especially wonderful.
62. "Witches Chant '98" by Inkubus Succubus is an incredible version of this chant.

of your vocals, feeling the energy rise and feeding it with your chant. Keep your ritual focus in mind. Increase your passion and vigor; feel the energy building higher and higher. Continue singing until you feel the peak approaching and then send it off with a deliberate gesture, perhaps a shout. Other than the chants I mentioned and others you can easily find with a bit of a search, you might try chanting the vowels (sometimes called "toning"). With the OM and vowel chants, take a deep breath then make the sound on the exhale, extending it as long as you can, stopping only to inhale again. (I especially like OM for group work as the different lengths of exhalation create a deep resonance.)

Dancing to raise energy requires a decent amount of space and enough privacy that you won't be disturbed. Start by breathing deeply, centering yourself, and bringing yourself to the present moment. Focus on your goal/intention/desire. Start dancing however you feel most comfortable to music you have chosen because it suits your mood and the needs of the ritual.[63] Keep your ritual focus in mind. Listen deeply to the music playing, and physically dance faster and with more intensity. Increase your passion and vigor; feel the energy building higher and higher. Continue dancing until you feel the peak approaching, and then send it off with a deliberate gesture, perhaps a throwing motion of your arms. Your dance does not need to be intense; you can raise energy while sitting. Use repetitive gestures and concentration to build energy. As well, walking in a clockwise circle will raise energy. Keep your focus on your ritual intent, and start walking. Gradually increase the pace until just before your energy peaks. To release, you might jump into the center of the circle and push the energy up and away with your arms.

2. Silent Meditation

Silence can be powerful because it forces us into a new paradigm; we are so dependent on speech. The energy raised will be gentle and the peak not so high, but it still retains its power. At its simplest, you start with a transitional statement ("I now offer up my silence" or similar). Using silence will be remarkably similar to a focused meditation, so using a focal point or a deliberately planned pathworking will help build energy. Start by breathing deeply, centering yourself, and bring yourself to the present moment. Focus on your goal/intention/desire. Breathe into your focus and feel the energy build. Release on the exhale.

---

63. I really like the work of Gabrielle Roth for dance/energy work.

3. Pathworking/Guided Meditation

Also called guided meditation, in pathworking a voice (the director) leads you into a trance state and guides you on a specific journey in which you are still connected to the physical world, and at the end, leads you back to waking consciousness. Within the framework of pathworking, there are two modes for the director: passive and directed. In a passive pathworking, the director provides the barest outline and information, allowing the meditator to fill in as much information as possible. This is an ideal approach for getting a lot of information from the meditator's unconscious. The script is full of general statements such as, "you are walking in a cave" and "the Crone speaks to you," but the meditator's imagination fills in the details. A directed pathworking describes everything in detail to produce a specific effect. The script will say, "You walk into a cave. The air is dry and flinty; the ground under your feet is a thin layer packed hard over the stone."

The following are advanced-level techniques for raising energy.

4. Yoga

Kundalini Yoga was popularized in the United States by Yogi Bhajan in the late 1960s to enhance ordinary life while exploring altered states of consciousness without drugs.[64] Yoga involves the awareness of breath (pranayama) and thought processes, in addition to a series of postures (asanas) designed to stretch and strengthen the body. As it is traditionally practiced, yoga is often combined with aspects of progressive muscle relaxation and meditation. Keeping the attention on a goal while engaging in a repetitive series of asanas to raise energy is challenging but rewarding. The two techniques I suggest are sun salutation and a seated breathing asana.

Sun Salutation

Breath is a significant part of this sequence. Movement from one pose to the next follows either an inhalation or exhalation of the breath. You can control the pace of the sequence by altering the number of breaths in each pose; just make sure to move to the next pose on the correct breath. Continue doing the

---

64. The topic of yoga is too wide to explain in any detail. I recommend Dianne Bondy's *Yoga for Everyone: 50 Poses For Every Type of Body* (London: Penguin/Random House, 2019) for a good introduction.

complete cycle of postures, building energy, and maintaining your focus on your goal/intent until you feel the power peaking, then send onward with an exhalation.

Start by breathing deeply, centering yourself, and bringing yourself to the present moment. Focus on your goal/intention/desire.

1. *Mountain Pose:* Stand with your big toes touching. Lift all your toes, let them fan out, and then drop them down, creating a wide, solid base. Bring your weight evenly to all four corners of both feet. Feel your feet and the calves root down into the floor. Widen your collar bones and make sure your shoulders are parallel to your pelvis. Your neck is long, the crown of your head rises toward the ceiling, and your shoulder blades slide down the back. Your hands form a prayer position in the middle of your chest. Take four deep breaths (approximately 30 seconds).

2. *Raised Hands Pose:* Inhale and bring your arms out to the side and reach up. Press the palms together, keep the arms straight and gaze up toward your thumbs. Slide the shoulder blades down the back.

3. *Standing Forward Bend:* Exhale and fold forward from the hips, *not* from the back. Bring your fingertips in line with your toes and press palms flat, using a cushion or other support if you can't reach the floor. Engage the quadriceps muscles of your thighs to open up your hamstrings. Bring your weight a little bit forward into the balls of your feet so that your hips stay over your ankles. Let your head hang.

4. *Half Standing Forward Bend:* Inhale and press your palms or fingertips into the floor beside your feet or into your shins if you can't reach the floor. With an inhale, straighten your elbows and arch your torso away from your thighs, finding as much length between your pelvic bone and navel as possible. With your palms or fingertips, push down and back against the floor or your shins and lift the top of your sternum up (away from the floor) and forward. You might bend your knees slightly to help get this movement, which will arch your back.

5. *Plank:* Exhale as you step your legs back until you are in a plank position, shoulders are over the wrists, and your whole body is in one straight line. Press your forearms and hands firmly down but do not let your chest sink. Press back through your heels. Keep your neck in line with your spine and broaden your shoulder blades.

6. *Downward Facing Dog:* Inhale as you walk your feet up until you are in an inverted V position. Place your palms on the floor just above your head, which is hanging down. Move your shoulder blades away from your neck and engage the quadriceps strongly to take the weight off your arms, making this a resting pose. Take four deep breaths (approximately 30 seconds).

7. *Standing Forward Bend:* Exhale and step or jump forward. Bring the fingertips in line with your toes and press palms flat, using a cushion or other support if you can't reach the floor. Engage the quadriceps muscles of your thighs to open up your hamstrings. Bring your weight a little bit forward into the balls of your feet so that your hips stay over the ankles. Let your head hang.

8. *Mountain Pose:* Inhale and straighten, lift your arms out to the sides and up, reversing the swan dive to return to raised arms pose. Exhale and return arms to your side.

End with savasana, or corpse pose: Lie down on your back and close your eyes, letting your feet fall out to either side. Bring your arms alongside your body leaving a little space, and turn your palms to face upward. Relax your whole body, including your face. Let your body feel heavy. Let the breath occur naturally, and stay here for several minutes.

To come out, first begin to deepen your breath. Then move your fingers and toes, awakening the body. Bring your knees into the chest and then roll to your side and get up. You should feel deeply relaxed.

Breath is a significant part of this sequence. Movement from one pose to the next is always with either an inhalation or exhalation of the breath. You can control the pace of the sequence by altering the number of breaths in each pose; just make sure to only move to the next pose on the correct breath. Continue doing the complete cycle of postures, building energy, and maintaining your focus on your goal/intent until you feel the power peaking, then send onward with an exhalation.

Seated Breathing Asana

Start by breathing deeply, centering yourself, and bringing yourself to the present moment. Focus on your goal/intention/desire. Spend 1 to 3 minutes on long, slow abdominal breathing. Raise your arms and extend them at a 60 degree angle with palms flat and facing upward. Continue the abdominal breathing for 1 to 3 minutes. Extend your arms horizontally to the sides with the wrists bent upwards and the palms facing away. Continue the abdominal breathing for 1 to 3 minutes. Bring your hands together and clasp them at the sternum with your arms pushing your palms together. Continue the abdominal breathing for 1 to 3 minutes.

5. Sexual Stimulation

While challenging for a beginner, this is a powerful technique with the added bonus of being fun to practice. The basic idea is to stimulate your sexual organs while maintaining your concentration on a goal.[65] Build your working in your mind, then release and expel all the energy in conjunction with your orgasm. Deliberately using your breath to control the rhythm of your sexual excitement while visualizing the outcome of your working adds intensity. If with another person, there must be active and absolute consent and agreement between participants about how to raise energy and the goal of the working.

6. Binding or Flagellation

Binding or flagellation/scourging are different ways to practice blood control and have a long history of ritual use.[66] Flagellation, the deliberate application of pain by using a whip, scourge, or other strapped implements, almost

---

65. "Sexual organs" refers to your entire body, not just your genitals. Stimulate what feels good and works for you.

66. "The ritualistic use of the whip was practiced in various Greco-Roman and Egyptian cults, namely, the cult of Isis, Dionysus, the Thargelia Festival, or the Roman festival of Lupercalia." "Flagellation," in *Religions of the World: A Comprehensive Encyclopedia of Beliefs and Practices*, ed. Gordon B. Melton and Martin Baumann (Santa Barbara: ABC-CLIO, 2010), 1119.

always conjures up images of sexual dominance. It has a "nasty" flavor, which is a shame as it is an effective method for altering consciousness. Binding (using cords or similar material to restrict blood flow) is a little less known outside of specific traditions but is just as effective. Ideally, these methods are combined with meditation and breathwork. Binding *requires* at least one other person present as it is too dangerous for most people to practice alone. Self-flagellation has a long and honorable history of use, although I do not recommend it for a beginner.

7. Drugs or Alcohol

Drugs and alcohol will put you in an altered state, and some will allow you to access energy. At the same time, however, they are the most likely to take away your focus and will, making your ritual pointless. There are some circumstances for ritual under the influence, but I just can't recommend this technique—and certainly not for regular practice.

Raising Energy Pattern

The basic pattern for energy raising is:

1. Starting—It often feels awkward to get started as it's usually a deliberate shift in tone and focus within the body of the ritual. Let yourself find the pattern you want to use, and don't be afraid to start over if it doesn't feel right. (Deity doesn't expect perfection; it expects intent.)

2. Building—This part of the working should feel like everything is going well. You know what you're doing; you're in the groove, and it feels good. If you are with a group, this part can take a long time as people find their way into the energy and begin to add their own.

3. Peak—This feels fantastic. The energy is flowing, and you know it's time to send it off, so you do. In my experience, you want to send the energy just before it hits the absolute peak because there is a tiny moment between when you decide to end it and send it. You can see the top of the rollercoaster's apex, and by the time you send that energy, you're there. If you wait until you are at the peak to send the energy, you're over the edge and starting downward. It

is perfectly acceptable to send the energy just a smidgen late, but if you can continue to work with the energy, allowing it to wane a bit and then bring it back up again, you can head for another peak. That said, it's exhausting, and I do not recommend it for beginners. Just know that it is a possibility you might explore at some point.

4. Release—Send that energy off in the manner best for how you raised it. I like to send it with a shout and a throwing of my arms up and out. You might also make a simple pushing gesture or even a deep exhalation. When you release, send every bit of power raised with as much intensity as possible.

5. Return—Raising energy should be fun and exciting, but don't lose sight of why you are doing it and know when to stop. When you've sent the energy on, it's time to return to a calmer, steadier place and let the energy lower as well. Your working isn't over; you've still got things to do in your circle.

Activity

The next time you light a candle for a party or dinner, do so while focusing on how fun (intimate/cozy/etc.) the coming evening will be. Journal how well that worked.

The next time you blow out a birthday candle, consciously make a wish—Journal how it turned out.

SHIELDING AND PSYCHIC PROTECTION

You might wonder whether anything unpleasant can happen if you work magic. Working magic is as safe as walking city streets or driving a car. It is entirely possible that bad things can happen, but if you take care and look before leaping, the likelihood is minimal. It's your responsibility to be centered, confident, and compassionate when you enter the circle. If you work from that place, you will amplify those qualities in your life. Perhaps because of my training in Muay Thai, I see Witches as a kind of spiritual warrior. We do not provoke a battle but learn to be deft at safely diffusing threats, often using the others' energy against themselves.

There are dangers in the astral realm and working magic, the most common of which is psychic attacks. A psychic attack is the perception of energy or an entity that intends you harm on a spiritual or physical level. Most attacks aren't genuine, and those few that are real are often unintentional. Some people choose to use their harmful energy to direct their anger, fear, or frustration onto another, a genuine psychic attack. When the attack is unintentional, it is usually from a person who lives in a negative mindset most of the time. Their "bad vibes" build up gradually until they take on a life of their own. Some environments are laden with this harmful energy; it's just part of the overall background.

Harmful energy can manifest as bad dreams, unusual physical pain, losing critical objects, or many accidents. Some curses manifest as a sudden illness when otherwise healthy and no other environmental factors (allergies, stress, etc.).

A bad dream, even several, doesn't mean you are the subject of a psychic attack, and cussing out a driver who cut you off in traffic isn't an attack on them. A *pattern* of bad dreams perhaps with ongoing, repeated themes, may be an indicator of harmful energy in your life (directed at you specifically or not). The most important thing is to be self-aware and check that the source is external, not your energy rebounding badly upon you. It is always helpful to ask, "why is this coming to me?" no matter if the source is external or internal.

One specific group of people unwittingly cause attacks because of their nature. Known as energy vampires, these people unconsciously drain others of vitality and emotions. The term is overly dramatic and lacks compassion. (That said, I don't have a better one to suggest. We don't need special terms for people with allergies, either.) Many, if not most, energy vampires are unaware of how they drain others. They feel depressed in some fashion, and being with others turns that around gradually, so they feel more cheerful and energetic. This type of person doesn't quickly recharge from an internal source, which is a subtle difference and requires a great deal of self-understanding and awareness.

Specific unwanted energies take on a kind of personality; we call them entities. These entities are unsettling, like scavengers (which they often resemble, energetically speaking). Scavengers play an essential role in a healthy ecology, but you don't want to live with one. When you first do magical work, entities probably won't take much notice of you. As you build your power, you will come more and more to their attention, kind of like standing under a light with a dimmer sWitch—the more you practice, the brighter the light shines, and the more clearly you are seen. An ongoing spiritual practice will keep them away, and they will eventually lose interest in you unless you work without shields or something that sets up an energetic flare.

Some entities are worth knowing, and the best way to recognize those is to make a joke. The ones you want to cultivate a relationship with will laugh; the ones you want to avoid will get angry, as laughter removes their source of power. Nasty entities know that fear focuses your attention and produces a lot of excess energy—a bonus for them. The best way to get rid of them is not to be afraid. Easier said than done, but, like Harry Potter's boggles, laughter renders them harmless.

The last source of a psychic attack is yourself. If you genuinely believe you are under psychic attack, the universe may just go ahead and create one for you. For this, self-awareness is your solution.

Other than self-awareness, the best way to keep yourself clear of bad vibes, harmful energy, energy vampires, and nasty entities is to create a shield. Creating a shield is a fundamental protection/comfort/defense, as if you are wearing a Circle. Ideally, your shield is flexible and semi-permeable, moving and growing with you, expanding, and contracting with your energy level.

Creating a Shield: Planning

Before taking this step, take the time to consider the details of your shield. What shape will it take? What color (if any)? What materials will you use to build it? Shapes often start simply and then get more complicated as your skills increase. Will your shield be round, spherical, cylindrical, squared, cubed, oval, or some other shape? I've heard of shields made from every color of the spectrum and the same for textures: from brick walls to puffy cocoons to steel spheres and laser force fields. Whatever makes sense and feels protective to you is what you want to use. No matter the form or shape, make sure to keep it semi-permeable, leaving you open to receiving positive energies while still providing protection.

Creating a Shield: Cleansing

Your shield is a permanent part of your being, and it makes sense to make sure you don't have any nasty energy attached to you when you build it. So, the first step is to start with cleansing; discussed earlier in this chapter.

Building the Shield: The Process

Once you've decided what your shield will be, visualize it around you in the form you've chosen. The first time, this will take a while; I expect you will spend at least 10 minutes getting it solid and clear to your inner eyes before stopping for the day. Repeat this daily for a week, shoring up any weak points you come across. Check your shield once a week for the next month, strengthening as needed. After that, check on your shield as needed in addition to formally at least once a year. Once your shield is well-established, it's self-sustaining and maintaining. Eventually, the only times you'll need to be aware of your shield is at its yearly housecleaning, when you think of an improvement, or when reacting to a threat. Here is a shielding visualization I was taught years ago that I still use.

Sit or lie down in a comfortable position and do relaxation and breathing exercises to become centered within yourself. When you are completely relaxed and "in" your body, imagine a bubble of light around you. It may be egg-shaped or round, or whatever makes the most sense to you. The light may have a color or texture. (For some, it may appear as water or smoke.)

Notice how the shield is not static but moves. It may pulse in rhythm with your heartbeat, or your breath. Look all around the shield and notice if there are places that are different thicknesses or brightness. You want to smooth these places out. Your shield is entirely under your control, and to smooth out these areas, see your energy flowing into, or out of, the affected areas. It won't be perfect at first, but will grow easier with time and practice. However your shield appears, imagine it smooth and even all around you. If it's too thick, you'll feel cut off from the life force of Nature, too thin and you'll be affected by the energies of too many others. Enjoy the sensation of being able to experience the energy and have it refresh and engage you in positive ways. Feel how lightweight your shield is and how it protects you.

Repeat daily until your shield is constant.

Maintaining the Shield

Once you've established a shield, it will power itself from your energy. You can reinforce it—in crowds, for example, or when encountering a person with nasty energy. You will want to regularly review it for cleansing and maintenance. In the beginning, I recommend reviewing your shield at least weekly, although if you are often in high-stress or emotional situations, daily is not too often. The following is a technique for shield maintenance.

Sit or lie down in a comfortable position and do relaxation and breathing exercises to become centered within yourself. When you are completely relaxed and "in" your body, take a look at your shield. Notice if there are shapes that seems to be sticking to your shield or if anything is penetrating it. (These may appear as cords.)

Visualize your shield pushing those shapes out of it, squeezing from the inside out, forcing them away. Watch as your shield heals itself after they are pushed out and feel how much more comfortable you feel as a result.

If a shape won't budge, imagine a glove of light covering your dominant hand. Using the glove, reach out and pull the shape from your shield and watch it dissolve in the light of your glove of light. When you no longer need it, allow your glove to melt away, ready to reappear if needed.

Cords

Cords—energetic connections to people and sometimes places or things—are not necessarily something you have to do anything about, and I recommend saving any cord work until you are very comfortable with energy work in general.

Most cords are positive, connecting you in mutually beneficial relationships to lovers, parents, your children, siblings, close friends, long-term co-workers, and anyone with whom you feel a deep and positive connection. These cords often connect to you in the area around your heart; energy flows between you and the other person in an energy exchange that is positive, loving, and supportive. Some cords siphon energy from you, often unconsciously and without malice, for example, a former lover or past relationship you've outgrown. Some signs of unhealthy attachments include:

+ Depleted energy levels
+ Feeling lethargic, depressed, or inexplicably sad
+ Feeling stuck or unable to make decisions
+ Obsessively thinking about another person
+ Getting sick often

+ Seeking comfort in unhealthy habits and addictive behaviors, such as smoking, binge eating, drinking, drugs
+ Over-emphasis on seemingly healthy habits, such as over-exercising

Removing unwanted cords can be simple or require repeated attempts, so start with the simplest techniques and work your way into the more elaborate methods as needed. Dissolving a cord creates a significant shift in your energy and is a very powerful, healing experience. Be proud of yourself: it takes strength and courage to take ownership of your life and your energy.

The simplest method is to take a salt-water bath or swim in the sea. Salt cleanses your energy body and allows you to return to a state of balance. While in the water, imagine the unwanted cord shriveling up and disconnecting from you.

A more elaborate method is to write a letter that formally ends the relationship. Write out everything you might say to the other person—be authentic, don't hold back! If you're angry, allow that anger to flow out of you as you write this letter. This is your space to feel your emotions and release them, not monitor your behavior or judge yourself for how you think and feel about the person or the situation. Once you've written the letter, tear it up into pieces and either toss it in the trash (and take the trash out immediately) or safely burn it. Energy is released through your hands and your mouth. Writing down your thoughts and feelings releases them rather than keeping them close to you.

The most elaborate method is to cut the cords in ritual. To do so, create sacred space and invoke the appropriate deities. While in ritual, visualize the individual and the connection between the two of you. Visualize holding a pair of scissors or a knife. With intention, visualize cutting the cord between you and witness saying:

"I now sever and release any and all energetic cords that do not serve my highest good. I release you and I release me from these binds."

Watch as the cord recoils back into both you and the other party. Take a moment to anchor the experience by feeling the recovery of energy and thanking the other person for the role they have/do play in your life. See your shield healed, smooth, and shining. When you are ready, thank Deity for assistance and close the circle. After you've finished the cord removal process, give yourself the time and space to rest and rejuvenate. Drink extra water and take a nap or go to bed early if you need to.

You may notice that after removing a cord, the person will reach out to you either physically or in your dreams. This a clear sign that the removal worked.

Protecting Your Physical Space

I admit that I secretly laughed at all the hippies talking about bad vibes when I lived in the commune as a child.[67] The idea of bad juju seemed weird and flaky. Time is proving them far too right; there is a ton of bad energy all around us, and the more we interact with the public, the more it gets stuck on us, like a layer of grime on the side of a building. These external energies can affect our mood, thoughts, and actions. Far too many of us carry sadness, worry, fear, and anger around all the time, and these energies transfer to others. Taking time to cleanse yourself and your space feels good on lots of levels, like a shower. The easiest cleanse is to add salt to water and rinse your hands, the soles of your feet, maybe your face. If you haven't done a cleanse in a while, you may be surprised at how good you feel afterward.

When you clean your living space, add salt to the water used. It can be tremendously energizing to give your space a thorough cleaning. Sprinkle it on carpets and down drains to freshen them. Place bowls of non-iodized salt around the house to capture negative energy, but be sure to change the salt every twenty-four hours.

Using incense with cleansing properties can assist in general cleaning when you don't have time to get out the wash pail. Some good options include rue, nettles, and thyme. If smoke is a no-go, try essential oils warmed in water over a candle or mixed with some vodka and sprayed into the air. Good essential oils to use for this are sandalwood, lavender, and frankincense.

Need to clear energy on short notice? Make noise! Ring a bell vigorously, clap your hands, and play loud music to clear the space quickly. Pay attention to directing the sounds into corners and dark spaces, where energy tends to get trapped and stagnant.

For long-term passive protection, look at charging items in your physical space. My house has several protective items, each protecting an entrance, a

---

67. I'm not exaggerating, it was called the Circus and was in Berkeley, CA.

door, or a window so that no evil can enter. Some ideas you might consider for your own space:

+ Folk items such as a *nazar* (the blue glass eyes from Turkey) or a mezuzah (the Jewish decorative case with a small piece of parchment inside)
+ A poster or image that faces the entrance—a wolf's stare can be very protective
+ Crystals or stones under your doormat
+ A live plant with protective properties (I like rosemary) near your front door.

These ideas can be adapted to almost any living space, no matter how small.

Using energy physically and mentally is a normal part of our everyday lives. Doing so with consciousness and intent is one way the Witch carves out their path. We do best when creating a life in which we cultivate stillness (even when there is only time for a quiet breath and pause while on the toilet). In the craziness of our mundane lives, being able to raise a shield against the bombardment of negativity seems like an excellent idea.

Having finished this chapter, you are now spending time daily, relaxing, meditating, doing various visualization exercises, grounding, shielding, and experimenting with one or more energy exercises. Keep up these practices!

Activity

Practice shielding—your goal is to be able to shield within thirty seconds from a cold start. Track your progress in your Book of Shadows. What images (objects, colors, etc.) work best for you when shielding?

Chapter 8

TOOLS OF THE CRAFT

*I am the most powerful tool I will ever wield. It is my responsibility to use
my energy, thoughts, and will to wield magick wisely!* [68]

Tools! Some Witches say we can't live without them; others wonder if they are
needed.

Sometimes it seems that we're supposed to go out as soon as we've decided
that we are a Witch and spend a whole lot of money on tools and accessories
because otherwise, we aren't "real" Witches. But others will say with equal passion that a "real" Witch needs no tools at all. Who's right? By now, I think you
know my answer: no one and everyone. Part of the problem arises from the
confusion in using the word "tool;" it tries to cover too many aspects and thus
serves none well. There are two main types of tools: physical and spiritual.

PHYSICAL TOOLS

Anything we use in life has the potential to be a magical tool. Our books, cars,
frying pans, musical instruments, computers, and even toothbrushes can help

---

68. From my Book of Shadows, circa 1999.

us function and improve magically. Whether you are using the ancient cauldron or a blender, one thing is obvious: we need to treat our tools with respect as we would partners. If we think they are our slaves, they will perform lifelessly: obediently perhaps, but without joy. If we spend the time to get to know them deeply and care for them, they will become partners in our magical workings and enhance our performance. They will become our teachers, allies, and friends. The amount of personal energy we invest in tools is, after all, what makes them become magic. Just remember that tools are visual, symbolic aids that hold no power of their own, just what we put into them.

There seem to be two schools on the creation, care, and feeding of tools; I call them the "ceremonial magic" and "kitchen Witch" perspectives. From the ceremonial magick perspective, the mundane is always to be kept separate from the sacred. If you use tools consecrated for magickal work for mundane activities, you will dissipate their energies or "contaminate" the tools. Therefore, you should choose tools and equipment carefully; consecrate and store them in particular ways, only using them for their ritual purposes. For example, discard leftover wine from a ritual rather than using it for dinner the next night. Deity imbues all of creation for the kitchen Witch, and everything is sacred (there is no "mundane"). They use whatever is at hand that works: kitchen knives, this morning's cereal bowl, the family salt, etc. They recognize the sacredness of all life when using leftover ritual food for tomorrow night's dinner.

I work somewhere between the two and see little separation between "sacred" and "mundane"; they are two ways of thinking about the same things. My altar always has objects I use solely in magickal workings and is also supplemented with everyday objects. For example, I use a sugar dish, and creamer set passed down to me by my grandmother to hold my salt and water, but I often raid my spice rack for spell components. I also have no problem with using my ritual candles when the power goes out. I think of all of the physical tools as being two types: focusing and working tools.

Focusing tools include symbolic objects of the elements (athame, wand, candle, cup or chalice, plate or pentacle), gems and stones, deity images, and objects with personal meaning. They are also things that engage the senses:

+ Scents from incense or essential oils
+ Colors from candles, robes, altar cloths, images

+ Sounds from music, chants, poetry, vocalizations, drumming
+ Tactile stimulators from things that produce different temperatures and textures)
+ Flavors from ritual food and drink

These tools keep your attention focused on the purpose of the ritual, engaging your subconscious and aligning it with your conscious mind. While preparing your ritual space, everything but the purpose of your working recedes. Working tools to include might also be used in focusing but have a more practical aspect. They are knives, scissors, thread, pens, paper, cords, cloth, salt, water, and everything needed. Divinatory objects such as runes, scrying mirrors, tarot and other card decks, I Ching wands or coins, and pendulums are also in this group.

Before we go any further, let me make one thing clear: every person beginning to do serious, focused work in Witchcraft needs at least two tools (the athame and the chalice), although four are ideal. One of the requirements for accepting the Second Degree within JaguarMoon is that you own a tool representing each of the four elements—air, fire, water, and earth. I feel *that* strongly about it because they will focus you in a way that, while possible without them, will require a lot more time and attention. That time and attention are better spent on other aspects of magical education and exploration. One student of mine put it very well: if I am gardening, I can do all of the digging with my hands, but it's easier to use a spade (or a shovel).

Athame

The old favorite and most common magical tool is the athame. There are many ways to pronounce this confusing word: some say *ath-ah-may*, others say *ath-ah-mee*, either seems accurate.

Traditionally, the handle is black and the blade is sharp on both sides. The athame is usually not used to actually cut, but instead, direct energy raised during rituals. It also "cuts" an opening into the astral realm when casting sacred space. Any pointy object can be an athame, including your finger. I've used a letter opener, my finger, a pen, and even quartz crystal, all with varying degrees of effectiveness.

The athame is the primary working tool of the craft and represents the will, the magical power of the Witch. The edge of the athame represents our ability to make clear distinctions and to reach a firm conclusion. The point represents the power of focused action and the will to act decisively. To use the athame, attune your energy field to the energy of the metal blade and let the metal resonate with your will. Doing so allows you to use the energy of the metal for casting the circle and cutting the openings, reserving your energy for those things which only you can do.

An athame is a projective tool representing freedom of action and is associated with the element of air although some traditions associate it with fire instead of air.[69] If you use incense to represent air on the altar, the athame becomes the primary symbol of projective energy (traditionally, the God).

Air is the intellect; just as our minds "cut" through our dilemmas, the athame cuts through time and space as an extension of our magical intellects. It's not always pretty, of course. Our minds lead us to new revelations that can be painful to us (ignorance is bliss). That aspect of the intellect is expressed through the appearance of the athame as a weapon. In many ways, this tool is a catalyst that reminds us of the polarity between constructive and destructive thought and the undeniable truth that things aren't always what they seem, but at the same time, always connected like the two edges of the blade. The only way to reconcile the polarity of construction/destruction in your brain is to focus them on a common goal, the tip of the blade. The tip is where the real power lies. The black handle represents all things—all thought, experience, and perception—and moves it along the center of the athame to the tip where its power can be focused and realized.

Acid Etching

Lore has it that a Witch once had to make their athame by hand, but few have the knowledge to do so nowadays. Instead, most of us buy one and personalize it in some way.

If your athame has a metal blade, you can use acid to etch symbols or runes on it.

---

69. Traditionally, this was referred to as "masculine."

Materials needed
Isopropyl alcohol
Athame or metal you wish to etch
Paraffin wax
Long, sharp, nail or needle
Goggles
Vinyl gloves
Glass dish
Cotton swabs
Hydrochloric acid (HCL)

Note: Make sure you do this work in a dust-free and *very* well-ventilated environment with running water nearby in case of accidents. Wear gloves, long sleeves, eye protection, and consider an apron. Work with one side of a blade at a time. Choose a simple pattern to start with, or practice on a piece of junk metal. Keep in mind that one mistake is all it takes for your athame to have the wrong mark forever. Please make sure you know how to dispose of acid after you're finished—you can't just pour it down the drain. If any acid splashes on your skin, immediately rinse thoroughly under cold water. If there is a burn, seek immediate medical help, no matter how mild. If it gets in the eyes, again rinse immediately, and call the EMT. Do not ingest the acid or leave it where a child or animal could ingest it.

Instructions
Clean the blade with isopropyl alcohol and then cover it with wax. Let the wax cool.

Carefully etch the symbols in the wax. Be careful not to remove any more wax than needed to reveal your symbol.

Don goggles and gloves.

Pour a small amount of acid into the glass bowl. (Pour slowly without splashing. Do not use plastic or metal—both will dissolve.)

Dip the cotton swab in the acid and wipe over the blade where you've scraped away the wax. Move quickly but with confidence to cover the exposed areas.

The acid will work quickly, so keep an eye on the area you first swabbed. If you aren't sure, you can rinse it under cool water to check. You'll need to dry it before applying more acid carefully. When you like what's happened, rinse the blade thoroughly.

To remove the wax, I recommend freezing your blade, which will make the wax break off pretty well (you can use a dull edge, like a butter knife, to dislodge stubborn pieces). If that doesn't work, pour a bit of boiling water over the remaining wax and use an old rag to wipe the blade clean.

Chalice or Cauldron

The chalice or cauldron are receptive tools associated with the water element. Along with the athame, the chalice is one of the primary tools in the Witch's collection. It symbolizes regeneration and nurturing; it represents the gates of birth and death and is a symbol of abundance, emotion, and fertility. If you have both, the cauldron becomes the receptive symbol, and the chalice, water.

Although the chalice can be any material that holds liquid easily and delights the user, the cauldron is usually made of cast iron and has three legs. The shape of the cauldron represents Mother Nature, and the three legs the triple face of the traditional Goddess.

Water is all emotion; through the tool of the cup, we learn to control, understand, and then let our emotions go. In the act of putting our emotions inside of the chalice, we can observe them objectively. Then we can experience them by turning them around inside of us and then drinking them into ourselves to allow them to meld with the larger vessel of our body. In doing so, our emotions become something they were not before. The chalice offers its wisdom when we drink its contents or offer a sacrifice through libation, the pouring of its contents onto the earth.

Wand

Used for thousands of years in religious and magical rites, the word "wand" comes from the Gothic word *windan,* meaning "wind" or "bind," and the wand often binds the energy of the spell together. The wand directs energy, draws magical symbols during ritual, and is wielded to invoke Deity.

Wands are usually made of wood, although sometimes of metal (especially copper), stone, or other materials. I have two: one of stone (jasper, a fire-related stone) and another of wood, gifted to me by a special friend. Alive when it was a tree, the wand can be used in place of the metal athame when opening a portal. It represents action at a distance and directed energy flow.

Neither air nor fire creates wood but can shape it without destroying it, as in erosion or burning. One can light a piece of wood on fire and destroy it or add a solution to the wood to make it burn indefinitely without destroying it. It's up to you to use whatever creative or destructive method appeals.

If we are to see the athame as a tool of the element of air, then it stands to reason that we need a tool of fire, a purpose the wand fits nicely. We cannot use an athame to light our way—no chemical solution will make a good torch out of pointy metal—but we can use a wand as a torch. The wand can be used to bring warmth and creative inspiration into our lives without destroying it or altering its integrity and usefulness. (Anyone who has ever sat beside a campfire and gazed into its hypnotic flames knows what I mean when I say fire can bring creative inspiration).

For all of the joy that fire brings into our lives, it brings pain as well. The wand is an apt tool to symbolize its power. The wand can focus and direct power in a similar fashion to that of the athame. Its symbolic usefulness increases when a Witch uses a wand to direct the construction of the cone of power, somewhat like putting a pot of water over a flame. The power/water boils and eventually transforms because of the heat. When the cone of power is released, it's as if the steam races off to become what the Witch has willed it to become.

The wand is a projective tool associated with the earth from which it grew and is paired with the pentacle. I consider it one of the secondary tools that is vitally important; if you can only have two, it is not as necessary as the athame and chalice or cauldron.

Pentacle

Completing the quartet of primary tools is the pentacle. Made of any material, although natural ones are best, it is a flat circle, with a star drawn on the surface. The pentacle is a receptive tool of earth and is paired with the wand.

The circle has no beginning and no end, the star has five points, one point for each element and a fifth to represent spirit. The pentacle represents the ability of the earth to create life.

Earth is always there and seems to be stable, but it is ever moving, changing, transforming itself, and all within its realm. It is the most mysterious of the elements to a Witch because it is only one thing—itself—but creates all other things. It can do so rapidly, in the form of a volcano's eruption which can change the landscape, or slowly, like a river forms a canyon.

Just as the circle around the star holds all elements within it, the earth itself is that from which all elements are created, and the same place where all elements find their ending. It is a circle that has no beginning or end, save for the divine will of spirit seen on the very same star within the very same circle. The lines of the pentacle represent the interconnections between the elements and all things in nature. The circle enclosing it represents the wholeness and underlying unity of the world.

A Simple Tool Consecration Ritual

Items needed
Incense (in the east)
White candle (in the south)
Small bowl of water (in the west)
Small bowl of salt or earth (in the north)

Cast the circle. Say:

Before these spirits, I bring (name of tool) to be dedicated to the service of the Lady and the Lord.

Pass the tool three times through the smoke of the incense, saying:

By power of air, be thou purified.
Be thou dedicated to purity,
that all goals thou help achieve may harm none
and be for good of all.

Pass the tool three times through the flame of the candle, saying:

By power of fire, be thou purified.
Be thou dedicated to desire,
that all goals which thou dost help achieve may harm none
and be for good of all.

Sprinkle a few drops of water on the instrument, saying:

By power of water, be thou purified.
Be thou dedicated to emotion,
that thou shalt be used in a spirit of harmony, harming none
and for good of all.

Touch instrument to the earth or salt, saying:

By power of earth, be thou purified.
Be thou dedicated to steadfastness,
that my will be achieved without wavering, with harm to none
and for good of all.

Hold the tool aloft and say:

Lord and Lady, bless this instrument, let it be a vessel of productivity that
may be worthy to reside in circle with you.

Guard the works which come forth from it, that they harm none and be
ever in the service of Thee. Let it be so bound that no harm may come of it
to any being.

To thy service, I dedicate this instrument, that it and I may be long of
service to thee.

So Mote it Be!

Thank and say farewell to the Lord and Lady, then thank and say farewell to the elements (in reverse from North anti-clockwise (widdershins) to East). Open the circle.

Activity

If you do not yet have any tools, consider rectifying that. Having an altar and Book of Shadows is a good start, so consider adding an athame, chalice, and incense burner. Those, plus a candle, will give you representations of all four elements.

Consecrate your tools. You can use the ritual outline above or create your own.

Write in your Book of Shadows:

+ Is it essential for a Witch to use/have an athame? Is using a wand, branch, or other tools just as effective? Why or why not?

+ What do the different tools, as a whole, mean to you?

+ What tools do you own? Describe them and their history (Where did you acquire it? How? Did you make it?)

+ What tools do you want/need to acquire? Describe what you are seeking.

SPIRITUAL TOOLS

Along with physical tools are the spiritual ones, and thus, we begin to understand the necessity to develop tools of our own. Éliphas Lévi tells us that the four powers of the Witch necessary for successful magic are: to know, to dare, to will, and to keep silent; together they are known as the Witch's Pyramid. The exact quote is:

> To attain the SANCTUM REGNUM, in other words, the knowledge and power of the Magi, there are four indispensable conditions an intelligence illuminated by study, an intrepidity which nothing can check, a will which cannot be broken, and a prudence which nothing can corrupt and nothing intoxicate. TO KNOW, TO DARE, TO WILL, TO KEEP SILENCE, such are the four words of the Magus, inscribed upon the four symbolical forms of the sphinx.[70]

These four qualities provide an additional layer of symbolism and preparation in creating ritual and working our Craft.

---

70. Éliphas Lévi, *Transcendental Magic: Its Doctrine and Ritual* (London: William Rider & Son, 1923), 30.

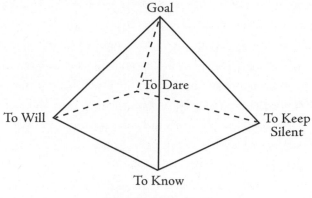

The Witch's Pyramid

To Know

"To Know" refers to gaining knowledge, most importantly if not exclusively, in order to know oneself. Being clear about what you want to manifest requires the alignment of the inner and outer self. Elementally, this principle corresponds to air and represents the Witch's reason/intellect/intuition/wisdom and other more mystical understandings. It has to do with the gaining of knowledge whether from books, teachers, or experience, and it includes anything having to do with organizing said knowledge: remembering, analyzing, dissecting logical reasoning, imagining, linking, and more. We see this in the many kinds of knowledge needed for ritual: remembering the words to invocations, knowing when to cast the circle, knowing what incense to use, remembering how it feels when one grounds correctly.

In Witchcraft, knowledge is power. No knowledge is wasted, and you will find that your fifth-grade Creative Writing class gave you techniques to create invocations, your Aunt Jean's gardening tips are helping you with your herb growing, or your tai chi class helped you understand centering. When we say, "Know Thyself," "Know your Craft," "Learn," and "Apply your Learning," we are speaking about knowledge.

To Know also means opening up our power to perceive, which allows us to free our minds of accumulated rubbish, to sort out illusions, falsehoods, and useless knowledge, and to become open to the vast possibilities our Universe contains. Within the craft, it is vital to accumulate as much knowledge in related areas as possible. Truth is everywhere, eager to reveal itself, but one must **know** to ask the necessary questions.

To Know means to acquire the knowledge necessary to carry out the task(s) you have set out for yourself. Be cautious and be confident that you have all of the information you need to do the job at hand properly. You must learn the fundamental reasoning behind magic and the tools used to create it to ensure the results you want. Is this difficult? It can be but many would also say that it's challenging to drive a car, bake a cake, or tie a shoe. As a Witch, you must *know*—absolutely and with certainty—what you are doing when it comes to magic; it's not a practice for mucking around. It may seem obvious, but it's incredible how many beginners take their studies for granted.

Research the kind of magic you are trying to do. For example, if you are drawn to use candles, first read about what other people have done with candle magic. What steps do they go through? You don't have to make your spell precisely like theirs, but if you notice that many people dress their candles with oil while concentrating on their purpose, (for example), it may be something that you want to try as well. (And don't forget to track the results!) Pay attention to magical correspondences as they can boost your energy—there is a reason I have a whole module on them. There are correspondences for colors, plants, animals, times of day, seasons, phases of the moon, and so forth. The more of these symbols you can incorporate into your work, the greater the focus of your energy will become.

Faith is a key aspect of To Know. It is the certainty that when we work our magic, it will succeed, that when we send our energy off with the cry, "So mote it be," we are stating that we can make things happen. Doubt kills magic. So we must develop our faith in our magic before we do it. One way to do so is to always speak the truth. Doing so reinforces that when we say something will happen, we know that it will.

Finally, having a focused imagination is key to working with this piece of the pyramid: the ability to see your desires and goals accomplished. It has to do with visualization and making what you have in your mind's eye reality. The more common term for this is creative visualization. If you cannot see the outcome you desire, you cannot create that reality.

Activity

Commit to never speaking falsehood, to never stating something will happen if you are not sure that it will. This isn't about telling lies or deceiving others; it's about not repeating something you are not completely sure is accurate. Don't press "send" on the meme about the kid wanting holiday cards in the cancer ward; don't tell your mother her hat looks great. Instead of telling a friend you will see them on Tuesday, tell them you are planning to see them. Of course, you won't be 100 percent accurate (I still call Pluto a planet, darnit!), but you are creating a life in which you speak only truth.

I recognize this is difficult, if only because most of us live in a society that prefers glossy and pretty to gritty and real. But difficult does not mean impossible, and becoming a being of integrity is a deeply valuable skill.

To Dare

"To Dare" refers to the willingness to put your Will into action, to go beyond normal boundaries, and to have total faith in your ability to reshape your reality. Elementally, "to dare" corresponds with the element of water and represents the Witch's emotions. This piece of the pyramid encompasses the acts of facing fears, especially with regards to doing magic. In magic, we dare to experiment with what we have learned so we can gain more experience. We dare to meet the gods and interact with them. We dare to deal with the darkness inside.

This is not to say that we don't feel fear or aren't supposed to feel fear—that would be foolish. The idea is to feel our fear and examine it so it can be dealt with. The more we try to hide our fear, the more power it gains over us. As the old saying goes, "Where there's fear, there's power." Instead, we must dare to tear ourselves loose from accustomed habits and conventional beliefs. We must dare to overcome our ignorance. In this way, we build the inner strength so necessary in Witchcraft. Any emotion brought into the circle will be increased and multiplied. Give strength to your courage by facing your fears and accepting them as a part of yourself.

"Dare" is a word that denotes the passion and desire to believe in yourself in a manner that makes you confident you can achieve your goals. It is nothing less than eliminating doubts from your mind and setting yourself on a solid ground of faith in your skills and beliefs. You must always stand proudly and stoically for what you believe in and revel in the fact that you leave no stone unturned and no possibility unvisited in your search for respect for your beliefs, rights, and powers.

You must **dare** to practice magic. You must use knowledge you have gained to create your rites and spells, often the hardest part of practice for new Witches. But the reality is that you never stop learning.

To Dare is to have rock-hard faith in our ability. To do magic, you must believe in magic and its power. According to Donald Michael Kraig, "Magic is the science and art of causing change to occur in conformity with will using means not currently understood by traditional Western science."[71] To achieve this, you must believe in yourself and your magic; without this belief, your magic is useless.

Activity

For a week, find one outrageous, unusual, alternative answer to every problem that arises. Large or small, make your solutions as fun as possible.

To Will

"To Will" refers to having an awareness of being in harmony with the universe and aligning your purpose with that which is greater than you are. Elementally, "to will" corresponds to the element of fire and represents the Witch's will, discipline, and skills in the arts of magic and life. In the mundane arena, it means keeping your life in good order, remembering promises and following through on your commitments. Magically, this refers to the will to see a spell or ritual to its completion, keeping the intent clear without becoming distracted. This is concentration, discipline, and drive as well as having the enthusiasm for doing the ritual at the outset. Admonitions to keep our thoughts and deeds in good order and breathe and eat correctly belong here, although the act of living within all the pyramid's dictates could fall under this piece of the pyramid.

Because we are the product of our thoughts and actions, the development of our magical will is vital. Willing is an astral feeling; no physical tool can be charged without the power of disciplined will. Without a will, you cannot cast

---

71. Donald Michael Kraig, *Modern Magick: Twelve Lessons in the High Magickal Arts* (Woodbury, MN: Llewellyn Publications, 2010), 10.

or defend the circle, the elements remain lifeless, and the God and Goddess live only in myth.

To Will is having the ability to concentrate and focus your need, knowledge, and desire in such a manner as to make something happen. You must be in control of yourself and your surroundings so that you can make your wishes come true in a positive and powerful way.

Once you decide to practice magic, you must be strong enough to **will** the spell into reality. The fear of failure or a spell backfiring is always there, creeping into the young Witch's mind. If you have adequately prepared, you will lose your fears. ("What if nothing happens?") This is important when doing magic because what you are doing is shaping the world around you to work in harmony with yourself and your well-being. You're creating your environment, shaping and molding it as an extension of the person you are and the person you want to be.

However, Witches are humans too, and we'll eventually make a mistake, no matter how hard we try. It is entirely normal, so don't fret when one of your spells goes awry. The wise Witch records it all in their Book of Shadows and then later reviews the workings to learn from the experience.

Activity

Choose a commonly used word, such as "the" or "we." For a week, do not use that word. Force yourself to consider every utterance, spoken and written, so that you avoid using your chosen word. If you do or must use it, commit to doing something mildly difficult as punishment—twenty push-ups, no dessert, no TV, whatever causes you pain. Ignore the desire to give yourself an exception "just this once."

To Keep Silent

"To Keep Silent" has been interpreted in many ways, all providing critical, valuable perspectives. There is the silence steeped in knowledge, regarding all magical work as hidden treasures, each a gem that might lose its luster if boasted about or shared with non-Witches. When something is a mystery and requires earning knowledge to understand it, it has more power; responsibility lends its energies.

Elementally, "to keep silent" corresponds with earth and represents the Witch's ability to restrain the ego. Perhaps after doing all the other things necessary to master the magical arts, you want to say to any who will listen to how wonderful you are. Resist the urge to toot your own horn—doing so dissipates your profound personal energy. It takes energy to mew wondrous phrases on your capacity to achieve, and that energy is energy gone. Energy saved is energy that can be used for much better results than the satisfaction of hearing your own voice.

This piece of the pyramid is often interpreted as keeping secret the knowledge of Witchcraft, membership, and places of meetings, etc. But silence represents the still point within. Meditation and maintaining a positive frame of mind come under this heading.

We also encounter silence for safety's sake. Although we have emerged from the Burning Times, this world is still full of intolerant and frightened people. A vow of silence serves as a reminder that those who wish to be open about their beliefs must be careful not to breach the confidence of others who may not wish to be as open for personal reasons.

Last, there is the silence of inner stillness. Only in this form of silence can one find the perception of the eternal and bring about its manifestation through the self. Some have said that silence is listening to the Divine Wisdom speaking within the heart. I know that when there are decisions to be made or an answer is needed that seems to elude me, I seek the truth within the silence of my higher self.

In many traditions, Witches keep silent about their magical workings in the belief that speaking about their work dissipates or diffuses its power. They also believe talking about their magical work can allow others to interfere with the outcome. I personally believe silence is the most potent power you can have in your magical toolbox. After all, *you* are the master of your thoughts but also the slave of what you say. This practice is not absolute, and many Witches talk openly about their workings. I encourage you to experiment and track whether keeping silent about your workings leads to better results in your Book of Shadows.

Witchcraft is steeped in secret; much of what we do is based on discovering the secrets of nature and the universe so that we can better work in harmony with its energies. If you work with an established group, part of your initiation and training will include the revelation of specific pieces of knowledge. Many of us take a secret name that is never revealed outside special rituals. Many of us also make vows never revealed except to Deity. In these circumstances, secrecy does good things for the group and the individuals. Our oaths are a kind of voluntarily accepted, cooperatively worked, and binding spell.

Warped people—abusers and predators—can twist secrecy into dangerous practices, and not just in Witchcraft. Christians have their Alamo, Berg, Jeffs, Koresh, and too many more to list here, and do I dare mention the horrifying institutional secrecy and cover-ups of the Roman Catholic Church? The sad fact is that any leader can use their power and position to hurt others, and they often cloak it in secrecy. In a path where we espouse an attitude of "many paths, no one true way," it is too easy for a predator to excuse themselves and their actions as their path and, therefore, no less valid than others. Witches pride themselves on their tolerance and open minds, which is generally good, but even these attitudes need moderation. It's essential to keep in mind that most predators depended upon secrecy because it protects them from being revealed.

We'll look at red flags and warning signs later. For now, know that secrecy can be powerful but is not without the possibility of danger.

Emphasizing the development and integration of all of your tools—physical and spiritual—is the basis of all magical workings. When we do this, we ensure the growth, effectiveness, and evolution of ourselves as individuals and as Witches.

Activity

When you do any form of magic, do not talk about it. Write about it in your Book of Shadows, but do not share it with anyone else. Consider never saying anything about it at all or only after it has successfully concluded.

Bonus Materials: My Ritual Log

This is the log I have been using since 1996 to track my ritual workings. The three boxes on the bottom are for the three-rune reading I do with each ritual.

Date:

Weather:

Moon Phase:

Zodiac Sign:

Energy Level:

Emotional State:

Health Status:

Purpose of Ritual:

Ritual Notes:

Outcome/Timeframe:

Rune/Card 1	Rune/Card 2	Rune/Card 3

Ritual Log

Chapter 9

CREATING SACRED SPACE

You must have a room, or a certain hour or so a day, where you don't know what was in the newspapers that morning, you don't know who your friends are, you don't know what you owe anybody, you don't know what anybody owes to you. This is a place where you can simply experience and bring forth what you are and what you might be. This is the place of creative incubation. At first, you may find that nothing happens there. But if you have a sacred place and use it, something eventually will happen.[72]

The vast majority of us are not born into Witchcraft, and many of us find that the language of the sacred was beaten and burned out of us, its meaning lost in hypocrisy and intolerance. Similarly, many of us grow up with a distorted idea of what is sacred. We were told that this statue or that space was sacred and thus separate from us, other. We begin to redefine our spirituality by discarding old notions of what makes something sacred and create new paradigms. In doing so, our definition of sacred becomes "that which brings us closer to the Divine." It must be one of our primary goals, therefore, to re-establish our

---

72. Campbell and Moyers, *The Power of Myth*, 92.

relationship with the Divine. We began this with our altars and now continue it by casting a circle.

Think about the sacred nature of things in your life in light of the following:

1. Is it sacred because it is vital to our continued existence? Food, shelter, water, and clothing are the things we need to survive in the world—do you consider them sacred?

2. Is it sacred because we were told it is sacred? Like saints' bones and ancient scrolls, is it inherently sacred or externally designated as such?

3. Is it sacred because it reveals some aspect otherwise hidden from our self? Tattoos, stones, feathers, jewelry all meet this requirement.

4. Does emotional attachment confer sacredness? Does the monetary value?

Consider your thoughts and feelings about respect and reverence due to an object. Is there a difference between an item found on a walk and one bought in a shop or online?

Some items may appear ordinary but are far from it, like the feather you found the day after Eagle spoke to you or the stick from the tree at your parent's house that died. Their sacredness lies within the memory evoked. Just as with a journal, creating a collection of sacred things tells you about yourself. A grove of trees, a hiding place where we once kept our toys and games, an engagement ring, a necklace given by a dear friend—all of these things can be sacred relics just as imbued with the Divine as a fragment of a saint's bone or a sliver of wood. Our sacred objects can be utterly ordinary and commonplace because of their very nature. Sacred must cease to be separate, for we devalue things kept from us, and it must begin to mean something more, something different.

Activity

In your Book of Shadows, journal your answers to the following questions.

+ What personal items in your life are sacred?
+ How did creating that list make you feel?

CASTING THE CIRCLE

One of the hallmarks of Witchcraft is that we cast a circle before doing most of our rituals and spell work. The circle is where we work magic and connect with Deity through worship, defining our ritual area, encompassing all participants, and the altar. The word "circle" is utterly misleading; what we are creating is actually a sphere. To my mind, there are three core reasons for casting a circle:

1. To keep the unwanted out.
2. To keep energy in.
3. To create an altered state of consciousness.

Keeping the Unwanted Out

As we talked about in chapter 7, there are some energetic nasties out there—ghosts and demons—as well as wild stabs from the subconscious. Even nominally benign energies, such as strong emotions from other people in your home, regardless of their positivity, can cause static interference with your working. Their effect is real, and they can cause damage. When you are in a trance or meditative state, you are open to their harm and disruption. Although your shields will keep many things away, they are not perfect. The wise Witch will begin ritual practice by defining *precisely* what will and won't be allowed into their circle.

Drawing the circle establishes boundaries within your environment. Doing so creates a space in which nothing can enter except what you invite inside. In effect, you are saying, "Everything within this circle is under my control." Purifying the circle with incense or consecrating it by sprinkling salt and water at its edge further defines the borders.

Keeping the Energy In

Magical energy follows the same laws as all energy. Its natural state is to be in motion, either moving toward a point or away from it. When we cast a circle, we contain the energy and concentrate it temporarily. All energy varies in intensity and frequency, even more so between different planes. While the discussion of planes is larger than I can encompass here, especially since there are a lot of conflicting opinions, suffice it to say that many people believe there are at least three planes: physical (where we are), spiritual (where ghosts and other spirits are) and the etheric or astral (where Deity is). There is a logic to this similar to that found in dimensional science: we start with length, area, and then volume to incorporate the three dimensions we experience. The circle acts as a magical tuner that helps us modulate the different frequencies of the physical plane and the astral.

Creating an Altered State of Consciousness

In my early days of formal training, I got into a conversation with another student who told me she had been doing a lot of what she called "wishcraft," which is what happens when you do magic not-quite-consciously. It makes sense, right? Everyone has angry moments, times of desire or despair. Sometimes those things get mixed up with energy work without our being fully conscious of it. I know I've caught myself doing it. Wishcraft is not a problem only if you don't mind working sloppy magic, because working magic without conscious intention and direction is just that—sloppy. It also invites a lot of unintended side effects and harm. I'm a Witch who believes a part of our magic is the ability to hex, not just heal, but I don't support wishcraft. It's like firing a gun without looking to see what direction you're aiming.

Many of the things we use to assist us in the Craft are based on the psychic cues we associate with them. Tools help us focus on specific types of energy in specific ways. Ritual apparel (or the lack of it) and the use of Craft names puts us in a deliberately chosen mindset. Everything we do to prepare for ritual— taking a bath, lighting incense, preparing our candles, gathering the materials we will use—puts us in a ritual frame of mind.

When you cast a circle, you know that you will be manipulating energies while inside it; that manipulation is a significant part of its purpose. Casting a circle cues your mind, both conscious and subconscious, to get into an energy-working mindset. As you begin to cast a circle every time you work magic, manipulate energies, or intentionally put yourself in an altered state of consciousness, you begin to associate those types of behaviors with working in a circle.

The Psychology of the Circle

The casting of the ritual circle is a psychological construct as much as it is an energetic necessity. Borrowed from psychology, Witches view the mind as a three-part entity:

+ the Ego (what you think of as yourself),
+ the Superego (what goads you to improve), and
+ the Id (that which reacts only to desires, needs, and primal urges).

The id is not affected by reality, logic, or the everyday world. Deeply submerged within your subconscious, it cannot judge whether what it perceives is good, useful, or healthy. It is the ultimate infant, caring only about having its needs met *now*. In the energy lesson, I talked about how your subconscious reacts like a computer; the id operates on the same principle as what makes affirmations work.

When we do ritual, we are attempting to connect our three selves to shift energy and manifest our will. We begin by drawing the id's attention to what we want done and then explaining what we need simply and clearly. Repeating the instructions in a chant helps the id understand our goals, and rhymes seem to work best. The ego and superego understand that you are trying to program the id. Like a fussy child, the id's attention needs to be attracted: special tools and clothing gets its attention. Acquiring hard-to-obtain items, drawing symbols, using unique language all reinforce the id's impression that this ceremony is unique. Using organized, meaningful symbols speak to the id, reinforcing the goals you set.

CONSTRUCTING THE CIRCLE

There are several ways to cast the circle ranging from very simple to exactingly complicated. All methods require concentration, visualization, and a commitment to the belief that the circle is real.

We construct a typical circle by calling the quarters (more on this later) at each of the four points of the compass: east, south, west, and north. While you can start in any direction, start in the east for this lesson. The steps to casting a circle are as follows:

- Walk the boundary of the circle
- "Cut" the boundary with your athame or finger, visualizing cutting the circle out of physical reality
- Call the quarters at each compass point to guard and protect while the circle is cast

Optional steps might include:

- Lighting candles or incense
- Purifying or consecrating the space

Describing it almost takes more time than doing, so what follows is how it looks when JaguarMoon does ritual:

Second
Be it known that our Circle is about to be cast! Let those who desire attendance at this ritual gather in the East and await the summons Let none be here other than by their own free will in Perfect Love and Perfect Trust!

Lead
Mighty Mother! Stupendous Father! Strike this blade with light that I may cast the Magic Circle.

I conjure Ye, O Circle of Art, to be a Temple between the Worlds.

A meeting place of love, and joy, and truth (drawing a pentagram in the east)

A shield against all wickedness and evil (drawing a pentagram in the south)

A boundary between the realms of men and the Mighty Ones (drawing a pentagram in the west)

A rampart and protection that shall preserve and contain (drawing a pentagram in the north)

The power which we shall raise within thee (finishes in the east)

Wherefore do I bless and consecrate thee. So mote it be!

Lead
Colorful spirits manifesting within the night, seal our circle, hide it from baleful sight.

Four points square the Circle and weave the spell, east, south, west, and north, your tale do tell.

East is yellow for the break of day.

South is red for the heart's desire.

In the west is sea borne blue.

North glows green, the sacred briar.

Three times 'round our circles are cast.

Great Ones! Spirits from our Past, Witness, and Guard us fast.

So mote it be!

At this point we call the quarters, ending with:

Lead
The Circle is cast. We stand Between the Worlds, Beyond the Bounds of Time. In a place where Night and Day, Birth and Death, Joy and Sorrow meet as One. Our ritual may begin!

When we walk the boundary of the circle, we visualize and feel a stream of energy coming from our body and form a bubble. (For me it starts as a flat circle that I draw as I call the quarters and "snaps" open to form a misty sphere when I close the circle.) We stop at each of the four quarters to "prime" the energy found there by drawing a pentacle (for me, made of blue flame). If alone, close the circle. If with a group, leave the circle open, stopping about a yard before returning to your starting point so everyone can enter the space and then close it behind them. An alternative is to start drawing the circle after everyone has gathered, in which case just close the circle, no need to stop.

When we finish our working, we release the circle precisely opposite of how we cast it, turning the sphere back into a line, and then pulling the energy used back into our athame while thanking the quarters for their presence and protection.

Pentagrams

I'm sure you noticed that my fragment of ritual text included the phrase (*drawing a pentagram in the [direction]*). This is not a literal drawing, as with pen on paper, but a visualization of a star drawn in some way that incorporates that direction's energy. Each element incorporates both physical and energetic components and most traditions agree that each point of a pentagram has a specific correspondence, like the one shown here.

When we draw the fundamental invoking pentagram, it starts with the element of spirit, and so we start at the top of the star. From there, go down to the left, up to the right, across to the left, down to the right, and then finish where we started at the top. A banishing pentagram, used at the end of the ritual, starts at the lower left, goes to the top of the star, down to the right, up to the left, across to the right, and then finishes back at the lower left (see All-Purpose Invoking and Banishing Pentagram illustration at right).

Some traditions have a unique invoking and banishing pentagram for each direction. If so, it will almost always start with the point associated with the direction: Air starts at the left-most point, Water at the right-most point, Fire at the bottom-right point, and Earth at the bottom-left point. Banishing pentagrams begin at the point opposite to the elements' direction. See the figures on the following pages.

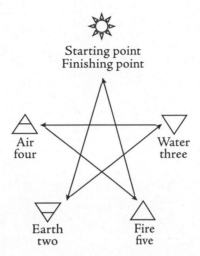

Starting point
Finishing point

Air
four

Water
three

Earth
two

Fire
five

All-Purpose Invoking and Banishing Pentagram

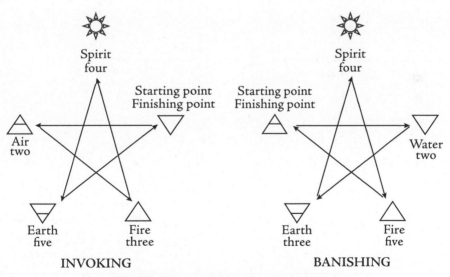

Spirit
four

Starting point
Finishing point

Air
two

Earth
five

Fire
three

INVOKING

Spirit
four

Starting point
Finishing point

Water
two

Earth
three

Fire
five

BANISHING

Air Invoking and Banishing Pentagrams

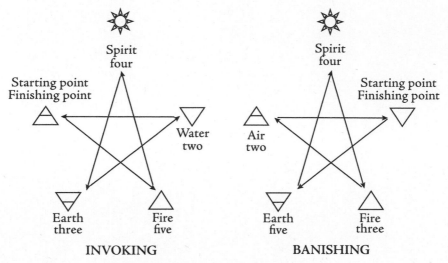

INVOKING   **BANISHING**

Water Invoking and Banishing Pentagrams

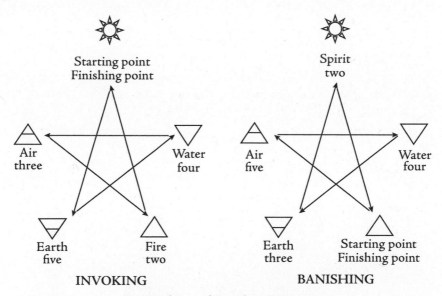

INVOKING   **BANISHING**

Fire Invoking and Banishing Pentagrams

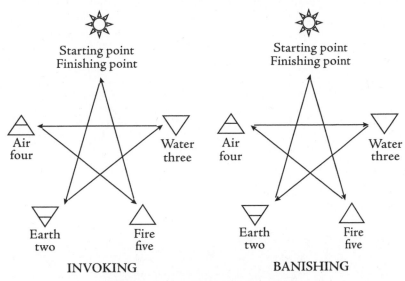

Earth Invoking and Banishing Pentagrams

Activity

As you grow more comfortable with visualizing and moving energy from previous lessons, add drawing invoking and banishing pentagrams to your practice. To do so, face east and contemplate the qualities of air. When you feel attuned to the energy of this direction, open your eyes and draw a large circle of energy in front of you with your dominant (also called projective) hand. Don't do anything with it; just let it hang in space for a few moments, then suck the energy back into your hand. Repeat until you can clearly see the circle in front of you. Gradually expand your practice by repeating with each direction. Then try drawing the invoking and banishing pentagrams instead of circles.

Activity

Cast a circle using a technique you create or the one provided. Spend time there—do not call quarters or Deity. Journal what you sense and think while you are in circle. Do this at least three times.

Cast a circle before you meditate. When finished, journal what the experience of meditating in circle was like; how it was or wasn't different from usual. Do this at least three times. In both exercises, the three times shouldn't be in rapid succession. Let the dust settle, so to speak, at least for a day or so before doing the work again.

Chapter 10
INVITING POWERS AND BEINGS

Working with others makes us much more than we could ever be alone.[73]

When Witches work magic, we almost always do so with others present, although few of them are human. This chapter looks at who we invite to work with us and why.

GUARDIANS AND ELEMENTALS

A fundamental part of a Witch's circle is calling the quarters. Even a cursory reading of publicly available ritual scripts shows going to each direction and welcoming some sort of being. Most commonly called airts, watchtowers, or guardians, these beings are associated with the four cardinal directions. Calling the quarters is two steps combined into one: recognizing a direction and recognizing a being in that direction.

Having cast the circle, we find ourselves standing "…between the worlds, beyond the bounds of time"—in other words, nowhere. The astral realm, the

---

73. John Wooden and Jay Carty, *Coach Wooden's Pyramid of Success: Building Blocks for a Better Life* (Grand Rapids, MI: Revell, 2009), 22.

energetic plane we access and connect with to work our magic is a vast, feature-
less plane. We work here because energy is more accessible to move than matter. But when we are here, we need direction, a connection back to the physical
plane.

Remember how I said that one reason for casting the circle is to state at the
outset that everything within the circle is under your control? Calling the quarters furthers that sense of control. In our ritual opening, we state the terms of
the circle: *"Four points square the circle and weave the spell."*

Then we define the directions in terms of their qualities:

East, south, west, and north, your tale do tell.
East is yellow for the break of day.
South is red for the heart's desire.
In the west is sea borne blue.
North glows green, the sacred briar.

In doing so, we are also greeting the elementals which combine all of the
qualities of that direction. Elementals do not have sentience but do have a kind
of rudimentary intelligence, and they have lots of energy. Elementals act as
lenses or tuners for the energy of their associated element. So instead of us
puny humans having to transmute the power of the universe into something
we can handle, elementals do it for us, regulating the amount of power flowing
into the circle.

Our id needs lots of imagery and associations to understand where it needs
to direct its attention. Deborah Lipp makes a great analogy: you can call a person by their first name (Lisa), and they might answer, but if you use their full
name (Lisa McSherry), they are more likely to answer. Best of all, if you get
descriptive (Lisa McSherry, who lives in Portugal, Lisa McSherry with the silver hair, Lisa McSherry, the organizer)—you will almost absolutely get their
attention.[74]

The elements within magical symbolism are the essential components of
all that exists. These four elements—earth, air, fire, and water—are simultaneously visible and invisible, physical and spiritual. All form the building blocks

---

74. Deborah Lipp, *The Elements of Ritual Air, Fire, Water & Earth in the Wiccan Circle* (St. Paul:
Llewellyn Publications, 2003), 109.

of all matter in the universe. Be careful not to think that these four elements are purely physical: Earth is not only our planet but also our foundation and stability.

There are four kinds of elementals:

+ The slyphs of air
+ The salamanders of fire
+ The undines of water
+ The gnomes of earth

Slyphs are flighty and elusive. They are creatures of intellect and are insubstantial. Their strength is information, and they lack emotion. If you want their cooperation, you must persuade them with logic. As creatures of air, they are placed in the east.

Salamanders are hot and destructive. They have no sense of caution or the consequences of their abilities. Their strength is primarily destruction, although they can be used to fuel creative output. If you want their cooperation, you must persuade them with your energy. They are creatures of fire and placed in the south.

Undines are fluid and emotional. They are creatures of emotion and intuition and have no patience with logic. If you want their cooperation, you must persuade them with your emotion. They are creatures of water and placed in the west.

Gnomes are solid and stubborn. They are creatures of secrets and endurance. You can't persuade them, but you can gain their cooperation by offering them respect. They are creatures of earth and placed in the north.

Working with the elementals combines many facets of your being, increasing your ritual or spells' likelihood of success. There are several associations for the four quarters that you can use to enrich your ritual work.

Element of Earth

The element most of us understand best, earth represents not only the physical earth but also the qualities of stability, reliability, dependability, abundance, prosperity, and wealth. It is upon earth that the other three elements rest.

Compass position: North

Season: Winter

Time of day: Midnight

Color: Green, black, brown

Gem: Rock crystal, malachite, moss agate, jade

Tool: Pentacle

Incense: Storax, dittany of Crete, benzoin

Astrological rulers: Venus, Saturn

Zodiac signs: Capricorn, Taurus, Virgo

Magical virtue: To Keep Silent

Attributes: Passive, receptive,[75] electromagnetic, cool, dry

Rules: Form, sensation, solidity, stability, containment, persistence, the body, manifestation, material things, birth and death, growth and decay, sustenance, gain, stones and metals, silence, graves, soil

Virtues: Stability, productivity, punctuality, commitment, responsibility, endurance, patience, firmness, calmness, practicality, pragmatism, strength, thoroughness, wisdom, sense of timing, imperturbability, endurance

Vices: Dullness, insipidity, restlessness, boredom, unreliability, misanthropy, impotence, tardiness, lack of conscience, melancholy, inertia, stagnation, hoarding of resources (including information)

Objects: All rocks and stones, metals, trees, pinecones, grains, nuts, comfrey, oak, ivy, oats, rice, rye, wheat, vetiver, mosses, lichens, nuts, heavy low-growing plants; most roots

---

75. Some systems will characterize this as feminine.

Beings: Wood nymphs, dryads, trolls, elves, gnomes, dryads, hama-dryads, elves, satyrs, pans, brownies, sylvestres, goblins, and tree spirits.

Animals: Wolves, mice, underground dwellers (moles, meerkats, etc.); all land animals

Places: Everywhere in nature, caves, fields, forests, caves

Element of Water

Water energy is the easiest to work with whether from a puddle or faucet. The energy is similar to air, not as physically destructive as earth or fire. This energy is most potent during a storm but is more valuable for reflection and the stimulation of psychic powers. Water energy can be drawn and used for dreaming, prophecy, divination, and cleansing the spirit.

Compass position: West

Season: Fall

Time of day: Sunset

Color: All shades of blue

Gem: Aquamarine, opal, pearl

Incense: Myrrh

Astrological rulers: Moon, Venus

Zodiac signs: Cancer, Scorpio, Pisces

Magical virtue: To Dare

Magical tools: Cup, chalice, cauldron

Attributes: Passive, receptive, magnetic, cold and wet

Rules: Emotions, love, sorrow, courage, the unconscious, psychism, sensitivity, tides, oceans, pools, streams, wells, womb, connection, caring, forgiveness, flow

Virtues: Devotion, compassion, serenity, trust, tranquility, tenderness, forgiveness, modesty, fluidity in creativity, receptivity, emotional stability, awakened psychic ability

Vices: Immaturity, dishonesty, self-indulgence, apathy, negligence, indifference, instability, moodiness, cowardice, vulnerability, pessimism, depression, infatuation, delusions

Objects: All forms of water (sea, river, well, etc.), blood, shells, coral, seaweed, river rocks, ocean stones, sea glass

Beings: Undines, water sprites, mermaids, limoniades, oreades, ondines, naiades, nereides, potamides, and sea nymphs

Animals: Dolphins, fish, whales, all creatures of the sea, serpents

Places: Oceans, rivers, lakes, marshes, pools, swamps, bogs, streams, rainforests, etc.

Element of Fire

Fire energy is the devouring power of intense emotions: anger, lust, and love. Just like the element itself, it is difficult to control, and it destroys everything it touches. When contained, fire energy reveals truth as well as fueling spells. It is most potent when out of control, as in burning buildings or forest fires, but it is practically useless in this form. A contained flame in a candle or hot coals is more valuable—more than enough for magic but not enough to overpower us.

Compass direction: South

Season: Summer

Time of day: Noon

Color: Red and orange

Gem: Carnelian, tiger eye, ruby, garnet

Incense: Frankincense

Astrological rulers: Sun, Mars, Jupiter

Zodiac signs: Aries, Leo, Sagittarius

Magical virtue: To Will

Magical tools: Wand, staff

Attributes: Projective [76], active, electric, hot, and dry

Rules: Will, force, energy, aspiration, purification, transformation, creation/destruction, courage, passion, intensity, enthusiasm, fervor, zeal, light, warmth, heat, liveliness, movement, power, passion

Virtues: Activity, creativity, courage, control, confidence, enthusiasm, passion, virility, chivalry, self-assertion, adaptability, growth

Vices: Gluttony, intemperance, lust, jealousy, irritability, anger, temper, hatred, envy, vindictiveness, egotism, self-centeredness, fanaticism, ruthlessness, destructiveness

Objects: Lamps, lights, candles, volcanic rock, all forms of fire (match, hearth, bonfire, etc.)

Beings: Salamanders, dragons, all felines, especially lions, lizards, scorpion, fox

Animals: Dolphins, fish, whales, all creatures of the sea, serpents

Places: Volcanoes, hearth and campfires, explosions, the desert

Element of Air

Air energy is more subtle than the other elements. It is in the air we breathe as much as the wind blowing over the hills. Air energy is light and can feel like any temperature when you work with it. It is most potent during a storm when lightning charges the air, and the wind blows fast. Air energy does not have as much physical power as earth or fire energy, but it has significant advantages. It is the energy of intellect, wisdom, and understanding. It also supports communication and friendship.

---

76. Some systems will characterize this as masculine.

Compass direction: East

Season: Spring

Time of day: Sunrise

Color: Yellow

Gem: Quartz, citrine

Incense: Galbanum, frankincense

Astrological rulers: Jupiter, Mercury

Zodiac signs: Gemini, Libra, and Aquarius

Magical virtue: To Know

Magical Tools: Athame, Sword, Censer

Attributes: Androgynous, active/meditating, neutral/conductive, warm, moist

Rules: Mind, intellect, reason, logic, intuition, abstract thought, knowledge, inspiration, movement, balance, harmony, justice, theory, understanding, breath, speech, wind, sound, communication, thoughts, meanings, concepts, nervous system

Virtues: Sociability, diligence, optimism, dexterity, persuasiveness, friendliness, health, knowledge, adroitness, kindness, cheerfulness, independence, joyfulness, lucidity, rationality, cleverness, adventurousness

Vices: Frivolity, boastfulness, absentmindedness, loquacity, rootlessness, distractibility, contemptuousness, intellectualization

Objects: Bells, incense, smoke, feathers, music, and instruments, poetry, songs, clouds

Beings: Faeries, slyphs, sprites

Animals: Birds, butterflies, all winged creatures

Places: Hilltops, mountain peaks, towers

Alternative Placements

Although the direction placement in the previous section is what I was taught, it is not necessarily the same as other Witches. The most common variance is to place air in the north, and Mike Nichols has done a masterful job of supporting that reasoning. To paraphrase his best arguments, air is in the north because:

1. In Celtic lore and mythology, air is placed in the north. (There, the four elemental/directional associations are referred to as *airts*.)
2. The majority of First People's cultures in North America place air in the north, symbolized by the eagle.
3. Most folklore aligns the seasons and directions such that winter = north, spring = east, summer = south, and autumn = west. When we look at the weather, winter's icy blasts could align with air and spring with earth as we see the blooming earth.

I can see placing the element of water in the east if you live on the East Coast of the United States, or in the north if in Chicago—follow your intuition. Spending time (a year would not be too long) tracking how your ritual work feels and manifests when working with the elements in different directions is a perfect exercise for deepening your connection with them.

Watchtowers

In approximately 5000 BCE after years of careful observation, the Sumerians noted that specific stars rose above the horizon only at certain times of the year, the four equinoxes and solstices.[77] They are:

+ Fomalhaut (in the constellation Piscis Austrinis) for the winter solstice
+ Regulus (in the constellation of Leo) for the summer solstice
+ Antares (in the constellation Scorpio) for the spring equinox, and
+ Aldebaran (in the constellation Taurus) for the autumn equinox

They called these fixed stars the Watchers and considered them to be eternally watching over human affairs and having the ability to allow humanity to

---

77. Francesca Rochberg, *Babylonian Horoscopes* (Philadelphia: American Philosophical Society, 1998), ix.

pass to the portals of other worlds. They built ziggurats (or "cosmic mountains") as temples.[78] Using "tower" as another word for "ziggurat" gives a possible origin of the term "Watchtowers."

Several thousand years later, the alchemists of western Europe associated the stars and directions with the four elements. Thus, north became associated with earth/Fomalhaut, south with fire/Regulus, west with water/Aldebaran, and east with air/Antares.

As an interesting side note, there is an obscure reference *in* chapter 6 of Genesis *to* the sons of God who had intercourse with human women, producing a race of giants:

1. When men began to increase in number on the earth and daughters were born to them,
2. the sons of God saw that the daughters of men were beautiful, and they married any of them they chose.
3. Then the LORD said, "My Spirit will not contend with man forever, for he is mortal; his days will be a hundred and twenty years."
4. The Nephilim were on the earth in those days—and also afterward—when the sons of God went to the daughters of men and had children by them. They were the heroes of old, men of renown.[79]

The Book of Enoch (composed in the third or fourth century BCE) describes the fall of the Watchers, the angels who fathered the Nephilim:

1. And all the others together with them took unto themselves wives, and each chose for himself one, and they began to go in unto them and to defile themselves with them, and they taught them charms
2. and enchantments, and the cutting of roots, and made them acquainted with plants. And they

---

78. John Lunquist, "The Common Temple Ideology of the Ancient Near East," Brigham Young University Religious Studies Center, https://rsc.byu.edu/temple-antiquity/common -temple-ideology-ancient-near-east. Accessed June 8, 2022.

79. "Genesis, chapter 6", King James Bible Online, accessed February 2, 2020, https://www .kingjamesbibleonline.org/Genesis-Chapter-6.

3. became pregnant, and they bore great giants, whose height was three thousand ells: Who consumed

4. all the acquisitions of men. And when men could no longer sustain them, the giants turned against

5. them and devoured mankind. And they began to sin against birds, and beasts, and reptiles, and

6. fish, and to devour one another's flesh, and drink the blood. Then the earth laid accusation against the lawless ones.[80]

Renaissance-era seer and alchemist Edward Kelley worked together with John Dee, a sage, to codify a system of magic that has had a profound effect on how modern Witches view the watchtowers. Kelley received messages in a process called channeling from a group of beings who claimed to be the same ones who had instructed Enoch. As Kelley received these messages, Dee wrote them down, and his writings came to become known as Enochian Magic.[81] Symbolically, it is represented by a large letter square divided into four parts by a large cross called "The Great Table."[82] The square is made of forty-nine tables, each with forty-nine rows and forty-nine columns of number and letter squares forming forty-eight "Gates of Understanding" (one gate cannot be opened). Dee called the four quadrants the watchtowers. Each watchtower grants access to twelve astral cities, and the watchers are their inhabitants. For the angels to leave their cities and enter human consciousness, the gates to the watchtowers must be opened. Formed when Adam and Eve left Eden, the four watchtowers guard the four extremities of the universe. The watchtowers contain all human knowledge, command the elemental spirits, have the power to transform things, and hold the secrets to all of humankind.

Many magical systems have distinctive versions of the watchtowers and watchers. Some see them as demigods, spiritual teachers, cosmic intelligence, or beings composed of light. However, they are not present at all in some eclectic (generally solitary) systems.

---

80. "Watchers," Academy of Ancient Texts, accessed February 2, 2020, ancienttexts.org/library /ethiopian/enoch/1watchers/watchers.htm.

81. Aaron Leitch, *The Angelical Language, Volume II: An Encyclopedic Lexicon of the Tongue of Angels* (Woodbury, MN: Llewellyn Publications, 2010), 2.

82. Called "The Black Cross" by Dee, who had colored it black in his manuscript.

In many traditions, the Guardians are regarded as real entities whose duties include working with the Witch, initiation into the mysteries, and gatekeepers to the portals of the Other Worlds. They are called upon for many purposes, such as spells involving healing, astral travel, and much more.

In the Wiccan Stregheria tradition, the watchtowers are called the *Grigori*, and they act as guardians to the portals between the physical world and what lies beyond the physical. The Grigori preside over rituals, allowing magical acts to establish themselves in the astral plane, or not. Seen as a stellar race, the Grigori are said to be the original essence behind the four archangels. Strega believe that the Grigori are escorts to the realm of Luna after physical death and that the Grigori watch over and provide them aid.[83]

Some magic workers only work with watchtowers for spells, not worship. Others call them to rituals as a way of giving thanks for their protection and guidance. In some magical groups, specific persons are always responsible for calling the guardian of a specific quarter and consequently develop a close bond with them.

Practical Usage

One way to think of the magical circle is having two portals: picture a circle within a square. The inner circle contains portals to the elementals in each direction, and the outer square contains the portals to the watchers.

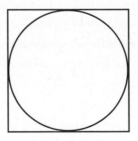

Squared Circle

For magical energies to flow between the physical and astral planes, the watchers and elementals act as the energy equivalent of transformers, moder-

---

83. Frater L, "Stregha," *Journal of the Western Mystery Tradition* no. 6. vol. 1, Vernal equinox 2004, accessed September 28, 2020: http://www.jwmt.org/v1n6/stregha.html.

ating and modifying the energy of the astral plane through the point of access thus making it easier for us to manipulate.

The watchers guard the circle and witness the ritual. Every time you perform a spell, you are sending out strong vibrations to the entire universe, which brings you to the attention of many beings—some of whom are not so well-intentioned. When asked, the watchers will protect you and hold the protection of the circle fast against attempts to break it down. The watchers witness and record the ritual permanently in the Akashic Records, a chronicle of every act in human history.

As you stand in the center of your circle facing your altar and tools when you work your magic in any spell or ritual, you become the spirit of the circle: the human, living connection with Deity. You, as a living being, are connected with the Divine and have the seeds of the Divine within you, and a part of you is within it. You can therefore draw upon this power, this connection, to draw down upon you all that you need to accomplish your work.

You become Deity, drawing that power or that mantle down upon you. You then focus your power through natural objects from earth, air, fire, and water (the building blocks of this existence) to manifest in this dimension your desired result. To do this, you must accept that you genuinely have this power, this ability. When you know this, deep down inside, the rest is history.

I hope you are beginning to see the patterns of life around you. Life flows in never-ending circles of associations and patterns. That is why our rituals are done in a circle, to remind us of the patterns we see enacted all around us in the great circle of life. Each of these patterns goes through a cycle that returns to the beginning over and over again.

Activity

Spend time working with one element for at least a week. During this time, you might:

+ Wear clothes in colors and styles that match the element.
+ Make offerings to the elements in distinctive ways.
+ Partake in activities that correspond to each element, such as:
  - Watch smoke rising from a fire, or stick of incense.
  - Watch an eclipse.

- Watch the clouds cross the sky.

- Float in the ocean.

- Sweat in a sauna.

- Stand in a warm summer rain.

+ Modify your behavior somewhat to emphasize each element's influence.

+ Engage in certain activities that put you in contact with the element.

+ Focus on the area of life that is the dominion of each element.

+ Spend the corresponding time of day with element (for example, rising at dawn to commune with air).

+ Keep a diary or journal of your experience in each element.

+ Copy the Elemental worksheets from the appendix into your Book of Shadows and complete them with information from this lesson supplemented by additional research or personal knowledge.

Answer the following questions in your Book of Shadows:

+ Who/what are the quarters?

+ What do they do?

+ How do they function?

+ Name three Gods and Goddesses associated with each element based on research or your intuition.

+ Name three animals associated with each element.

+ Are you drawn to one or more elements rather than others?

Extra credit: Read Mike Nichols's "Re-Thinking the Watchtowers" at Witchessabbats.com/site/index.php/other-articles/re-thinking-the-watchtowers and journal how his thinking does or does not make sense to you.[84] Would you contemplate shifting your practice to follow his suggestions?

---

84. Mike Nichols, "The Finer Points of Ritual: A Comparative Approach to Liturgical History, Theology, and Design," Internet Book of Shadows. Accessed May 11, 2020, https://www.sacred-texts.com/bos/bos632.htm..

INVOKING DEITY

Before beginning this lesson, you may want to review the work you did in the Basic Deity lesson, particularly your journal work regarding how you view Deity.

Most Witches acknowledge the glorious multiplicity that is our Deity. All genders, and none; all colors, and none. All expressions are represented and contained within our Deity. The Bible says that man was made in God's image, which is a useful way to go deeper into our never-ending exploration of what Deity means to us.

When we invoke Deity by Name or Aspect, we call upon a particular type of energy and consciousness. In doing so, we want to be as accurate in our invocation as possible. It's no good just choosing a Name because you read it in a book; that's kind of insulting. You want Deity to feel honored, not like an afterthought. Our invitation must be sincere, specific, eloquent, and from our deepest self.

When creating your invocation, spend a little time figuring out who you want to invoke. Be careful to pay attention to which aspect you want to invoke. For example, you may wish to call upon Hermes but as Hermes Eriounios (giver of fortune), or Hermes Dolios (craftiness), or Hermes Diaktoros (guide/messenger), or one of his other fifty-plus names. Or consider whether you want his Roman counterpart Mercury—there is a difference between the two. Just as in calling the quarters, calling on a name is good for magic, but being as specific as possible is better magic.

If you don't believe a specific name or aspect is needed or aren't comfortable working with one right now, it is always perfectly acceptable to call upon the larger umbrella titles of Lady and Lord. JaguarMoon usually invokes the Lady and Lord because we all worship different deities. Within the ritual framework, we might invoke specific aspects for their energetic qualities (gods associated with the sun during a Litha ritual, for example); we very rarely limit our rituals to one or two names.

It is wise to be descriptive, not just specific. Would you be more willing to spend time with someone who says, "Hey Lisa," or "Glorious Lisa of the Silver Hair?" Good descriptions create a synergy between Deity and you. Attention has an energy all its own—ever notice how you can feel someone watching you? Energy you put into your invocation in research, planning, writing, and finally speaking, call more strongly to Deity. Your description can be about physical attributes, such as Shiva's weaving hands or Lugh's beauty. It may include their attire or objects, such as Hera's peacocks or Ogun's ax. If it isn't already apparent, I strongly encourage you always to praise them. Typical terms are: excellent, glorious, mighty, beloved, lovely, dread, stern, and wise, but specificity is again your watchword. If the deity you call upon is most known for their kindness, perhaps call upon them as "the benevolent."

Finally, it is usually a good idea to let them know why you are inviting them to join you. Is it for worship? To witness? To guide or protect? To bless you or your endeavor?

What about "Drawing Down"?

You may have heard about drawing down the moon and are curious about what it is and when to do it. My short answer is: don't try this from a book. Drawing down is a kind of self-induced possession. To draw down the moon, you need to get into a state of deep trance, offer yourself to the Goddess *willingly*, have Her accept your offer, and then allow Her to enter. When done right, it is a profoundly sacred experience. When done wrong, it can cause a lot of psychic damage. The good news is that if you aren't ready for it, it won't work.

Invocation Examples

Here are several invocations you might use in your own work:

> **Goddess Invocation**
> *Gracious Goddess, you who are Queen of the Gods*
> *Lamp of Night*
> *Creator of all that is wild and free*
> *Mother of women and men*
> *Lover of the Horned God*
> *Protectress of all Witches*
> *Open our hearts, strengthen our loving bonds to one another*
> *Descend I pray*
> *With your lunar ray of power upon our circle here!*
> *So mote it be!*

God Invocation

Blazing God, you who are the King of the Gods
Lord of the Sun
Master of all that is wild and free
Father of women and men
Lover of the Moon Goddess
Protector of all Witches
Open our hearts, strengthen our loving bonds to one another
Descend, I pray
With your solar ray of power upon our circle here!
So mote it be!

Goddess Invocation 2

Glimmering Moon
Moon's Heart
Eternal One
Lady of the Animals
Lady of the Fields
Lady of the Waters
Dancing Child
Mother of us All
Thread Spinner
Diana
Astarte
Cerridwen
Move us
Touch us
Shake us
Bring us through
Heart of the World, we call to You: come!
So mote it be!

God Invocation 2

Bright Sun
Dark Death
Lord of Winds

Lord of the Dance
Sun Child
Winterborn King
Seed Sower
Grain reborn
Dionysis
Osiris
Pan
Move us
Touch us
Shake us
Bring us through
Horned One, we call to You: come!
So mote it be!

A typical full moon ritual invocation might be:

White moon mother, come to us as love to lover.
In the moonlight shining bright,
I call to you by will and right.
Magic and wisdom, secrets you bear,
honor I give you, knowledge to share.
Within this circle I have made a place,
be here with me and show Your grace.
Bright One, be welcome.
Horned hunter, come to us with joy and wonder.
You who offer death and return,
I call to you with hearts that burn.
Yours the law and yours the choosing,
and yours the wild hunt's grand career.
I welcome you freely, teach us not to be trapped within fear.
Horned one, be welcome.

If you wanted to use specific names, you might start by adding a line at the outset such as, "Glorious Goddess of many aspects." Note that the structure of the invocations mirrors one another, placing God and Goddess on equal terms. This equality reflects how many Witches view Deity.

Activity

Journal in your Book of Shadows your answer to these questions:

1. What is an invocation?

2. What is its purpose?

3. How is an invocation different from a Call/Release?

4. Is an invocation part of a standard ritual? Why or why not?

5. What is your favorite invocation? (If you don't have one, spend some time online looking for three new invocations that you like.)

6. Write an invocation. If you need help getting started, copy the structure of your favorite from question 5.

Chapter 11
CREATING RITUALS AND SPELLS

*Ceremony. Ritual. Sometimes formal, sometimes casual, but **always**, always precise in the intention.*[85]

We live in a world of ritual, often without seeing it enacted. From the small rituals of daily life to the once-in-a-lifetime ceremonies surrounding births, marriages, and deaths, ritual is a powerful element in human development. Ever since I was a small child, I have been drawn to the ritual aspects of our lives. Despite their use of English rather than Latin, Catholic services enchanted me with the magic of candlelight and sonorous music. As a teenager, I was aware (though dimly) that we sorted out our social status and marked our entry into adulthood through a variety of rituals while "hanging out." The legalized ceremonies of getting married and divorce placed those life changes into a broader perspective. As a Witch, my spell work and pure worship link me into a larger pattern tracing my roots back to ancient shamans.

When we look, we begin to find an extraordinary array of rituals in our everyday lives. In a glorious paradox, we are at the same time a culture cut off

---

85. Anne Bishop, *The Shadow Queen* (New York: Roc Books, 2009), 158 (bold in original).

from the ritual connections that held and guided our ancestors in fundamental ways. Many of the rituals of life go on outside of our awareness and intentions. Even the ones we pay attention to have lost their meaning as we go through the motions of what were once potent sources of inspiration and support.

Fair warning: I make only a fuzzy distinction here between ritual, ceremony, and spell work, often using the terms interchangeably. In general, I think of spell work as actions that elicit a specific outcome or change. A ceremony is a specific process undertaken consciously, while ritual is a broader category involving an element of divinity. Rituals may contain spell work but ceremony rarely does. Although I acknowledge the fact that ritualistic behaviors can, of course, be used to defend against anxiety or in attempts to gain control for the sake of one's ego needs, that is not what I am discussing here.

The keys to ritual are:

- Symbols
- Enactment
- Structure/format
- Containment/release
- A balance of intention and surrender
- Integration (conscious and unconscious, mind and body, discipline and wild, human and nature)

The use of symbols in a conscious, deliberate manner allows us to experience ritual in a way that helps complete dialogue between the conscious everyday portions of our psyche and the unconscious. Symbols encourage the unconscious to seek the deeper meaning of the ceremony. Dreams, artwork, guided imagery, tarot, runes, and other symbols give us ways to listen to the unconscious and to bring us messages, as well as color, scent, the feel of specifically chosen tools in our hands, or music all link us and provide intensified focus on the ritual's purpose. Ritual provides a means of profoundly affecting, and in a sense, fertilizing the deepest layers of our minds, speaking to our deep unconscious.

Ritual provides a way of acknowledging our relationship to each other, to spirit, and to the earth; it calls attention to our connections with the larger world around us. The substance of any relationship is communication, and in ritual, we listen and speak to each other and our deeper psyche. Celebrating the seasons or marking the phases of the moon, for instance, call to our attention our relationships with nature. Greeting the sunrise even if it is just a few spoken words or a bow to the east reinforces the understanding that we are a part of that sunrise and it is part of us. That moment includes both the sun climbing over the horizon and our experience of it combined, not as two separate events. The ritual of that bow acknowledges the web in which the sun and we are one. Lighting a candle when we sit down to a discussion communicates our intentions to act with integrity and openness and helps us listen to each other. Writing in a journal as a ritual rather than merely a way of taking notes about the day deepens it into a way of contacting our Selves in a more profound way.

In general, rituals encourage people to look for the more profound significance of their behavior. For example, you are not just lighting a candle when ritually lighting a candle—on a deeper level, you are also entering sacred space, affirming a wish or prayer, or reaching out to another who may or may not be physically present. The significance of lighting the candle lies beneath the physical actions. Such an act calls us to question or recognize its deeper meaning. We descend from the surface into the depths, and our next actions or words carry more meaning. The mind and the world settle and begin to sound a deeper resonance.

Ritual provides sanctuary in the sense of a safe place that is protected enough so that you can explore difficult emotions and also a place of worship where the deeper meaning of grief, rage, and despair are acknowledged. Those who are reluctant to share their feelings and insights begin to speak up; people who chatter to keep a "positive" front learn to honor the silence of their wisdom. Tears hidden in ordinary living are freely shed in the twilight of ceremony. Risks are less risky. Grief, rage, and despair can be as sacred as bliss and serenity.

Ritual also resolves duality and splits between surface and depth, head and heart, self and other, temporal and universal, human and nature, and sacred and profane. When we engage in ritual, the surface actions become the deep meaning: lighting the candle is affirming commitment to respect whatever is said in that space. We enter a place of deep community, and our essential connections are revealed. The planning and organization of the head becomes the sentiment of the heart and vice versa. The time-bound ritual actions become timeless and universal as we move in sacred space, and the potential arises to realize that the sacred lives in the profane and the profane is sacred, under its wraps.

RITUAL

Many of us who came to Witchcraft from other religions have minimal or even negative experiences with ritual. Religions of the book (such as Christianity, Judaism, or Islam) tend to see ritual as something watched, external, and minimally participatory. In contrast, ritual is core to the practice of Witchcraft, which is a very hands-on belief system—the word "craft" speaks to the practice as well as the process. One way we recognize each other as Witches is in our practices, what we do, not by what we believe. Witches actively assert and strengthen their connection to Deity, creating lives of physical, spiritual, and emotional richness.[86] One way we do so is through ritual. I think these words from Mike Nichols capture the importance of ritual perfectly:

> First of all, religious ritual is a human experience, a very universal human experience. It is as real as fear, and as important as love. It has a meaning of its own. It is not some sort of aberration or distortion of reality. It is an injection of new meaning into the reality around you. There is hardly a culture in the world that has not developed its religious rituals.[87]

I have written a lot of rituals and spells in my time, and I fully expect to write a lot more before I go into the ground. Most of the time it is fun and easy, but I've had many a student over the years get mired down on this lesson. My files have numerous rituals and spells gathered over the years. It's easy for me now mostly because I have done it so much, but in the beginning I spent way too much time writing drafts and discarding them. There have also been some spectacular ritual failures along the way! I remember with chagrin a ritual with

---

86. This seems like a good time to remind you that when I speak of Deity, I am including the perspective of those who consider themselves non-theistic.

87. Mike Nichols, "The Finer Points of Ritual: A Comparative Approach to Liturgical History, Theology and Design," Internet Book of Shadows, accessed May 11, 2020, https://www.sacred-texts.com/bos/bos632.htm.

such a muddled focus that while we were ostensibly calling upon Bast, all the symbols and imagery were appropriate for Hecate...not good.

Ritual empowers us by asserting that we are the physical embodiment of Deity (the life force present in all things) and thus are sacred. Ritual identifies our needs and helps us fulfill them. Creating personal rituals forces us to work through the reasons and motivations for each symbol used, making each unique and meaningful. Through ritual, we connect with, honor, and heal the deepest parts of ourselves, bringing our inner strength and wisdom to conscious awareness. Ritual allows us to evaluate and validate the physical and emotional transitions of our lives.

We attune ourselves with the natural cycle of life, death, and rebirth by marking life passages having to do with creating life, connecting our communities of blood and choice, and returning to the earth. In doing so, we affirm our place within the natural world and our inherent divinity. Modern Witchcraft is not tied to a heterosexual fertility cycle—instead it allows for the participation of all genders and orientations. Our focus is on personal experience, opinions, ideas, and feelings, not those of the people around us. Time spent alone and in consciously-constructed sacred space allows us to explore aspects of ourselves that do not surface in mundane spaces.

Whether our rituals mark significant life passages, employ elaborate structures, or are carried out within the repetitiveness of daily life, they celebrate the sacred within our lives and our connection with the sacred. Many of us overlook opportunities to create ritual to mark significant times in our life, thereby moving away from the possibility of sacred. Consider these ideas for ritual:

+ Grieving after a miscarriage or abortion
+ Preparing for surgery
+ Healing from a long illness or accident
+ Weaning a baby
+ Becoming a parent, or grandparent
+ Becoming an adoptive parent
+ Starting a new career (or job)
+ Staying clean or sober
+ Coming out

+ Divorcing (or separating)
+ Cleaning one's "nest" after the children have left home
+ Preparing to make love

Note that these rituals can be done by anyone involved in the event. A father needs to grieve as much as a mother after a miscarriage; both parties are healed by ritually marking a divorce. Ritual is for everyone.

Although ritual is defined by doing a specific action in a specific way, in a specific sequence, not every ritual is the same. If nothing else, your purpose will differ but your overall structure and format will be similar. In my experience, creating a ritual framework to be used consistently creates an expectation and sense of anticipation among the ritual participants.

A key element of ritual is the creation of an altered state of consciousness (ASC). The mental work we do, meditation, concentration, and visualization, all involve the conscious induction of an ASC, something I often refer to as being in a ritual frame of mind. The more we work with the same symbols and pre-ritual set up, the more those actions begin to become part of the ritual frame of mind. When we take on a name or invoke Deity in the ritual itself, we enter an ASC just as when raising power and going through a guided visualization or pathworking.

A former teacher once said that ritual is like meditation with props, which is a bit simplistic but speaks to the importance of the practice. If what you do in ritual touches you sincerely, then it is a success.

Are you feeling a bit nervous? Don't panic. It takes practice, but writing your own rituals and spells will give you so much more—meaning more power, more *magic*.

SPELLCRAFT

Spellcraft (or spellwork) is related to ritual but not defined by it. Spellcraft always includes ritual, but not all rituals include spellwork. For example, you might include a cord working spell within a ritual honoring the Egyptian goddess Neith, but the spell could also be done at another time. Spellcraft is a ritual act that uses your personal language of symbols—colors, scents, herbs, and objects—to manipulate energy to bring about a desired result. Spellwork is magic, rarely performed to connect with the sacred. Rituals also use symbols but are more likely to use what has been agreed upon within a larger community. Sabbat rituals, for example, use symbols from the culture being celebrated or the tradition of the ritual's origin.

CREATING RITUALS AND SPELLS

Your first step is to decide what you intend with the ritual. There are three types of rituals:

1. Worship: These include sabbats and any kind of holy days.
2. Recognition: These would be rites of passage, including Initiation.
3. Magic: These are the spells, of which there are three sub-types:
   - Summoning: Bringing something into your life
   - Releasing: Getting something out of your life
   - Connecting: Creating or affirming relationships with others, including Deity

Whatever your intention for the working, describe it to yourself as best you can—write it down! Be detailed and expressive. You need to be able to name and clearly visualize the result of your working accurately; without focus, your ritual or spell will not produce what you want. At the same time, avoid the trap of the sentence list, also known as providing too much detail with our description. For example, "I want a car that is blue, brand new, low cost, in perfect condition, and easy to find." Whew! Much better to say, "I want the perfect car for me." I find that speaking what I want to accomplish out loud helps me focus my intention. All words have power and are imbued with the energy we give to them. When full of our intent, words are a vital part of the working. The spell or ritual you write yourself is the most powerful; it grants you perfect focus on *your* wish and uses *your* energy. Of course, "know thyself" is critically important here; if you are so tied to details that you can't help but focus on the lack of detail as you work, it's counterproductive to do so. To the extent that you can get comfortable with it, try to avoid the sentence list.

Knowing the ritual intent, the *why* will let you answer the next step's questions. These are:

+ Who else will attend? The more people involved, the more possibly complicated the ritual.

+ Where will it be held? Location can strongly dictate what is and isn't possible. For example, if you want to hold it outdoors, you will have to plan for the vagaries of weather. (I guarantee that if it "never" rains, it will on the night of your ritual.) If indoors, can you find a space big enough? Do any participants require special physical accommodations? What about personal needs?

+ When will it be held? There are a ton of factors that can affect the timing of your ritual. If it is a sabbat, you'll want to hold the ritual close to that date and even more so if it is an esbat. Other timing factors might be:
  – Lunar (phase of the moon)
  – Astrological (a planet in a specific sign)
  – Menstrual (marking the onset of monthly flow or its cessation)
  – Religious (a day sacred to a specific deity)
  – Personal (a birthday, or the needs of participants)

+ What supplies are needed? These are things beyond the usual tools that you might need for the ritual. It might include: a lighter, candles, food, charcoal, incense, paper—anything and everything you will use within the circle. (I can't tell you how many times I've been chagrined to find out that the essential item I need was sitting just outside the circle.)

Raising Energy

This is a crucial element for most (if not all) of your rituals. Even rituals of worship could include a section in which you gift the deity with your energy only as a "thank you" for all they have provided for you. As you know from the energy-working lesson, there are many ways to raise and send energy. Which makes the most sense for your ritual?

Answering all of those questions may seem like a lot of work when you haven't even started writing the ritual itself! Doing the groundwork will make the writing go a lot faster and easier, I promise.

Ritual Core

Time to get to the writing itself. Most modern Neopagan rituals follow the same format to some extent:

1. Prepare yourself and the space
2. Cast the circle
3. Consecrate the space
4. Call the quarters
5. Invoke Deity
6. State your purpose
7. Do the work
8. Raise and send energy
9. Ground (often Cakes and Ale)
10. Bid farewell to Deity
11. Bid farewell to the quarters
12. Bring down the circle
13. Open the circle
14. Spend time in the afterglow

Some ground rules:

+ What you set up, you must take down.
+ The energy raised must be sent or grounded.
+ Everything you do on the upside (see Ritual Energy pattern illustration) is oriented toward and supports your ritual intent.
+ The structure is not the ritual.

The building and flowing of energy looks somewhat like a stairway up and then back down.

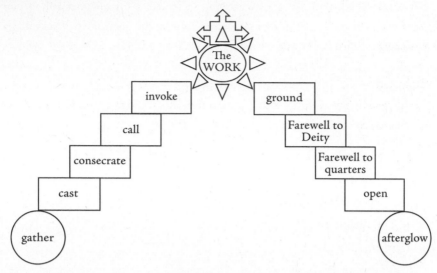

Ritual Energy Pattern

Prepare Yourself and Your Space

Deliberately, intentionally, cleansing the space and yourself before ritual is a good idea for many reasons. I suggest cleaning the space first so that when you wash up, you can go right into the ritual. And by cleanse, I mean literally: dust and sweep or vacuum the floor (the broom so long associated with Witches is handy here). Next, clean it energetically: use the smoke from incense or make noise to clear the space (such as a chime or bell). Scatter salt by itself or mixed with thyme, rosemary, frankincense, or sage. Hold the herbs in your hand and infuse them with your personal power to increase their effectiveness. If this seems difficult, think back to the energy-raising exercises, in particular, making a ball in your hand. Repeat that exercise, only place the herbs in your hand while you practice. Put yourself in mind of intending for the energy to reside in the herbs and you've got it! Refresh the space as much as you can, it makes a difference in how well the ritual goes.

While a bath is traditional, a shower works just as well. Water is a wonderful medium for taking away impurity. Let the water take away the day's stress and wash it down the drain. You can add salt and herbs to your bathwater, tie fresh herbs to the shower head, or fill a reusable teabag with herbs that soften in the warm water and can be rubbed over your body.[88] Visualize any negativity flowing off you and into the water, draining away through the plug hole. If you've had a tough day, salt mixed with your water will do an extra thorough clean. If you just don't have the time (and that's real), you can shift your energy by changing your clothes (shedding the day!) and anointing your third eye (located in the center of your forehead) with consecrated oil. Wafting the smoke from incense over your body, paying particular attention to your head, will cleanse you if you don't have access to water, as will imagining a strong wind blowing through you and carrying negativity away. You can also lie on the ground and let any negativity seep out of you and into the soil. Another way to shift your energy is by chanting. Holding a long OM sound can shift your energy intensely.

Do what feels right and gets you into a place where you are looking forward to ritual.

Cast the Circle

Enter your ritual space and mark the area you will make sacred. The circle is constructed from your personal power and is the place where you meet with Deity and encounter transformation. Casting the circle defines the ritual area and holds within it the power raised until it is sent off to do its work. It also shuts out distracting energies and negative entities. Although we call it a circle, it is really a sphere. If you can visualize it accurately, it can also be a square/cube, a triangle/pyramid, or any shape you feel is appropriate. A sphere is traditional mostly because it is the most efficient shape; all points are equidistant from the center.

There are several ways to mark out a circle for ritual:

+ Formed with cord or rope
+ Chalk on the floor
+ Objects such as flowers, pinecones, stones, shells, or crystals placed
+ Traced in the sand or dirt with a finger, wand, or athame—ideal for sea and forest rituals
+ Pouring a ring of some substance such as powdered herbs, crushed colored sand, or salt

---

88. A cleansing bath sachet may consist of equal parts of any or all of the following: rosemary, lavender, basil, thyme, hyssop, vervain, and mint.

The size of the circle depends on your needs. An individual generally needs far less space than a group, but dancing or doing something physical changes the amount of space needed. Mark the four directions with lit candles or other objects that make sense for the ritual.

How you cast the circle depends on personal preference and what feels right. The following is one way to do so:

Stand in the direction you wish to begin casting from. East is a good point as it represents the dawn, new beginnings, and the intellect. Feel the energy building within you, visualize it swelling and glowing. When it has resonated completely, hold your projective (dominant) hand palm down at waist level. Point your open finger towards the edge of the future circle. See and feel the energy flowing out of you in a stream of light. Slowly walk the circle deosil (clockwise) and push the power out into a circling band of glowing magical light. Visualize the circle expanding into a dome of energy surrounding the ritual area and extend the energy down into the earth to complete the sphere. When the circle is complete, break off the flow. Palm down, pull your hand back to your body and shut off the flow of energy.

If you wish, you may also use the appropriate tools for casting the circle, such as the wand, athame, sword, or staff to act as a conduit for the power raised and to help direct energy.

Call the Quarters

Calling the quarters refers to calling the guardians or elementals at the four cardinal directions. As you know from our lesson, these are guardians who are called upon to witness and oversee the rite and protect the sacred space from negativity or unwanted energies. They are also asked to lend their particular strengths to the ritual working. Depending on the tradition or your preference, they may be called Guardians, Keepers, Watchtowers, Airts, Mighty Ones, Archangels, and generically as elementals. Some traditions trace pentagrams to invoke and welcome them at each quarter, and others offer a salute with the athame or tool of that element. Each elemental realm has its spirits, rulers, and particular attributes. (See the Elementals lesson for more of this information.) There is no generic way to call a quarter. We make a direct connection between the elements and the directions and those same qualities within ourselves.

Invoke Deity

Deity is the honored guest at the party of your ritual. Invoking them is to invite them and welcome them to your sacred space for the celebration and worship. Witchcraft isn't about prostration and abasement; it's about having a relationship. Invoking Deity is mostly a matter of personal preference. Spoken word, dance, chants, poetry, gestures, and song have all been used to invite and welcome Deity into sacred space. Impromptu invocations in your own words can be more powerful, effective, and sincere than the most ancient of prayers. Invoking Deity requires a willingness to open yourself *to* Deity and be *with* them in circle in an atmosphere of perfect love and perfect trust. When we invoke Deity, we invite what is already present to be present with attention and intent.

Inviting Deity is a big deal—you want to be very clear about who you are inviting and why. If you don't want to use a specific name, it is polite to use appropriate honorifics, such as Lord and Lady, and suitable adjectives, such as magnificent or bounteous. (Genderless Deity needs no honorific but adjectives are advised.) Ask yourself why you want to call a particular deity. For example, if you are writing a ritual for the harvest, it might be tempting to do a web search to find a name and use that. But that would be like inviting someone to your party just because they drive a red car. Does the deity you want to invoke exist within a pantheon you typically work with—a relative of sorts? Have you spoken with them in meditation and prayer? If not, you'd be wise to start before the ritual. Have you researched the deity more than just a web search? And by "research," I mean going beyond everyday Neopagan books and instead looking through the myths of that particular pantheon so that you understand their personal story. Calling a deity with whom you've had no prior contact (even minimal) is rude, if not disrespectful. And what makes you think they'll even show up? If you want a response from them, it is best to establish a relationship with them *before* casting your circle.

What follows are the Deity invocations I wrote for a full moon ritual for social justice:

Mighty Goddess!
Fierce protector at the hearth
Stern dispenser of justice tempered by mercy
Strict Mother who teaches us the Lessons we must know.
We call upon Thee to bless our circle tonight

As we walk between the worlds
So mote it be!
Mighty Lord of swift Justice!
Bring us Your blazing sword!
Bring us Your fiery passion!
Help us find the spirit of Action, Deed, and Word
To best accomplish what we set out to do.
So mote it be!

State Your Purpose

I would say that the need for this is obvious, but I've been to a ton of rituals where the purpose is never stated. It's like holding a wedding but not letting anyone know why they are attending, even after they've arrived. Even a single sentence can be sufficient, and not having one will seriously undermine the ritual.

Do the Work

The body of the ritual happens here, the construction part of the ritual. It may start with a meditation, a conversation with Deity, or the re-enactment of a myth relevant to what you want to accomplish and the deity you've invoked. It may be a reading from an appropriate text or putting on a play by group members. This is also when you will carry out your spellwork: making charms and amulets, spell invocations, healing, and so on.

Rhyming isn't a requirement, but if you are doing spell work or raising energy, chanting it is an excellent idea, and I say this as a person who actively struggles with rhyming. Rhymes go straight to the part of your brain that responds to rhythm, symbols, and other nonverbal cues—that is, the part of your brain that produces magic. Other poetic tools like alliteration and assonance will work but typically not as well.

Once the mechanics of your construction or celebration are complete, it's time to move on to the next step: energy raising.

Raise and Send Energy

In practical terms, this is the magic, the point in the ritual where we use the movement of natural energies to affect needed change—we use our will to produce conscious change in our lives.

We cast the circle to retain the power we raise. When building power for a spell, Witches attempt to hold it inside their bodies until it reaches its peak and then release and send it toward its goal. It is challenging to retain all this power, so the circle holds it in until the time of release.

Energy can be raised in several ways. Again, this is a matter of preference; no way is more "correct" than another. Ways of raising energy include:

+ Dance and movement
+ Singing
+ Chanting and repeating mantras
+ Drumming
+ Drawing energy from all around

Once the energy has reached a peak or achieved its maximum capacity in a cone of power, it is released. This is usually done by forcibly stating or even shouting, "So mote it be!" although any directive phrase will work. Think of it as though you've been turning the key on a wind-up music box. At some point you can feel the tension in the key that says it won't productively turn any further. That's when you get to let the music play.

Ground

In some rituals, this is the Cakes and Ale stage, as eating is a great way to ground energy after ritual. Food is a manifestation of divine energy and eating a form of communion. Before you get to munching, make an offering of it to Deity in thanks for their attendance and participation in your rite. If you don't want to eat, you can also lay your hands upon the earth or floor and connect to the energy that way. Grounding balances your energy and resets you after ritual.

Bid Farewell to Deity

Just as you invited them, so must you also bid them farewell. Be polite: would you just walk out on guests at a party or kick them out? Mirroring the language of the invitation to join ritual, we thank them for their blessing and bless their leaving.

For example:

Lord and Lady!
Mother Bounteous and Lover Delightful!
We thank you for your presence tonight!
We have manifested our needs and know that they shall be made physical.
Gracious Lady, Fabulous Lord, Your blessing upon us is felt.
Go as you must.
Blessed be!

Bid Farewell to the Quarters

Just as you invited them, so must you bid the quarters farewell. Base how you bid them farewell on how you invited them to the circle.

For example, if you called them as:

Guardians of the East, Elementals of Air,
Muses of Inspiration and Creation
I welcome you to my circle tonight.
So mote it be!
You might bid farewell by saying:

Guardians of the East, Elementals of Air, I enjoyed your creativity tonight!
Thank you for your presence in my circle.
Blessed be!

Open the Circle

This is where you formally open the circle by cutting the boundary of it with your athame or fingers. If you cast the circle deosil (clockwise), you will open it widdershins (counterclockwise). Opening the circle formally marks the moment we move from ritual space, sacred space, back to the mundane world. Our intention, our magic, lies in the hands of Deity.

If you used the sample circle casting from above, you would open the circle by standing where you closed it. Feel the energy of the circle all around you and hold your projective hand, palm down at waist level, pointing towards the edge of the circle. See and feel the energy flowing into you in a stream of light.

Slowly walk the circle widdershins and pull the power back into you until you come back to your starting point. We like to say, "May the circle be opened, yet remain unbroken" at this point to formally mark the moment.

Spend Time in the Afterglow

A good ritual *feels* good when you finish. You'll have a feeling of accomplishment, a sense of satisfaction, or perhaps anticipation. Here's a tip: if you end up feeling drained, ill, or weary after ritual, you did too much. It's also possible that you may not have grounded well enough, so check that too. As a wise woman once said, "Remember, there is nothing that is not a part of the ritual, from the time people arrive until they leave."[89]

EXTRA BOOSTS FOR EVERY WORKING

What appears here is a personal collection of things I recommend happen with every magical working. It's far from a list of "musts"; more like, "try it and see" suggestion.

Clean your altar. I am mightily impressed with people who spend time cleaning and arranging their altar every day; I don't. Instead, I make a point of spending time there before every ritual. Experience has shown me that working with a dusty or cluttered altar tends to produce unfocused magic.

Purify. Different from cleaning, this is about taking the extra step to clean the energy of your altar, the space you will cast a circle in, and yourself. You might use smoke from burning herbs or incense, salt and water sprinkled over the space, a ringing bell, or even clapping hands to cleanse the space.

Center. Spend a bit of time before your working to ground and center. Get your energy into alignment with your intent and clear your head of any distractions.

Tune out. Unplug from all distractions. This includes the phone, TV, and anything that might break your concentration.

---

89. Wendy Hunter Roberts, "Creating Ritual: A Guide to Design" *SageWoman* no. 46 (Summer 1999): 33.

Add allies, thoughtfully. Think about what extras might be appropriate to your working to help you focus on the successful outcome: stones, herbs, colors, incense, oils, anything that makes sense to the intent of the ritual. There are lots of lists of correspondences for every kind of magic, and those can be a good starting point, but they are not as valuable as the correspondences that are important to you.

Work with the timing. Whenever possible, follow the natural energy currents. As the song paraphrases, there is a time for starting things (planting), for maturing things (growing), for reaping things (harvest), and for rest and planning. Magical workings for gain, increase, or bringing things to you, are ideally started when the moon is waxing (from dark to full), just as the waning moon (from full to dark) is best for magical workings of decrease or sending away.

Read it aloud. Words that look wonderful on the page can trip the tongue and mess up the energy you are raising.

For me, ritual is a journey on an edge between power and freedom. The potential of ritual is extraordinary and commands my most profound attention. As a leader, I naturally want to do ritual in a way that brings out the fullest potential. It is sometimes difficult for me to remember that worrying about doing it "right" only gets in the way. There is no predicting the outcome, but if my intention about the process is clear, the outcome seems to always take care of itself. Ritual calls me to balance care and surrender.

Let go of inhibitions, enter the sacred circle with respect, trust in your innate wisdom and the wisdom of your people and place, and experiment with an open mind.

THE POOL OF POSSIBILITY

When we do spells, it is vital that we strive for things within our reach. If we're out of a job and can't pay the rent, doing magic to own a Maserati is a poor use of our energy—we've got to be in survival mode! There was a time when I was so broke I had to choose between paying for the subway to get to work, and eating anything other than the sandwich I brought for lunch (I could get by on coffee for breakfast and shared dinner costs with my roommate). The magic I did during that time was focused entirely on successfully navigating the lean time. Although I was employed, it just didn't pay enough. I asked for a new job, and less than a month later was earning 20 percent more. That allowed me to start paying down the debt I'd accrued, so I asked for the strength to keep it lean. Carrying a charged stone for a year helped me make good choices about what I spent my money on, and I could see how well I was doing. That was when I started doing magic for a better future. I still don't own a Maserati, but I never wanted one. Instead, I own my home and retired in my 50s to live my best life.

Our magic goes amiss when we try to get things we can barely visualize, let alone manifest. It's a lot easier to start with small things and enjoy the success we have in gaining them. Such success empowers us to move on to bigger and better things. The more success you have, the larger the pool of possibility becomes, the more you will have within your reach. After all, nothing succeeds like success.

Activity

Journal in your Book of Shadows about the following:

+ What is the difference between a ritual and a spell?
+ Is it essential to give something of yourself (personal sacrifice) to be successful in magical workings? What kinds of sacrifices, if any, have you made in magical workings? Is a sacrifice different from an offering? If so, how?
+ How do you feel about mixing pantheons, correspondences, or systems?
+ Is it essential for a coven or any magical group to develop a "map" for ritual workings to be powerful and successful?

Write a ritual. Be as complete as possible and detailed as necessary, and include everything you would need to explain it to someone else. If this is your first time writing a ritual, remember that it does not need to be perfect. Take a breath and relax—you can do this!

Do your ritual; journal what worked and what didn't.

Bonus Materials

Spell Worksheet—this is a tracker I created years ago.

Spell Worksheet

Goal:

Date and Day: **Moon Phase:**

Candle Color: **Plant Ally(s):**

Stone Ally(s):

Correspondences and symbols used:

Words of Power:

Result:

Spell Worksheet

Bonus Reading

Ritual Theory and Technique, found at the Internet Book of Shadows, https://www.sacred-texts.com/bos/bos612.htm.

The Finer Points of Ritual: A Comparative Approach To Liturgical History, Theology and Design, found at the Internet Book of Shadows, https://www.sacred-texts.com/bos/bos632.htm.

CONCLUSION

Everything you've learned and journaled about is now a part of what you can confidently call your spiritual practice. My deepest wish is that you have a good sense of the foundations and have confidence in your practice. Ideally, you also understand that being a Witch isn't about having an environment full of crystals, feathers, and things. Nor is it about wearing "Witchy" jewelry, getting tattoos, or painting sigils on your skin. You know that Witches are of every color, race, gender, career, opinion, and attitude. That you are a Witch when you consciously align yourself and your life with nature and its energies, do the work to become a better person, and manifest a better reality for yourself and your loved ones, all in service of creating a better world.

As I polish the edits on this book, *Roe v. Wade* is in danger of being overturned, our former president and his followers are being examined for sedition, and children are still gunned down in their schools. Many of us have spent our entire lives fighting for the right to make decisions about our own bodies, the right to be with whomever we love, and even just the right to live. Witchcraft and other alternative spiritual practices have long been a tool for the marginalized and oppressed. In the United States many of our founding mothers, if you will, found their way to Witchcraft through feminist "consciousness-raising" get-togethers. They found that being together, sharing experiences, widening their circles of support, made them better people…and more able to create new ways to dismantle the patriarchal systems of oppression.

We know that with magic, we can align with the energy of the unseen world and improve the odds of creating real, positive, change in the world around us. As outsiders, we have a different view of mainstream structures that allows us to clearly see the problems with those structures. As outsiders, we can revel in doing what we think is best, not what we're supposed to do.

With magic, we understand how powerful we are.

With magic, we can make the oppressors afraid. More accurately, we can make them more afraid than they already are.

With magic, we can transform our own fear into anger.

With magic, we can change the world.

Take a moment (or a week!) to celebrate your accomplishments. Know that your future growth will build on the knowledge you've gained as you fully develop your practice.

> *Be the fire.*
> *Be the water.*
> *Be the air.*
> *Be the earth.*
> *Be yourself; all elements combined.*
> *Creating magic*
> *Living magic,*
> *Blessed be!*

—Lisa McSherry
Summer Solstice, 2022

ELEMENTAL WORKSHEET

Copy into your Book of Shadows and complete each section with the information you find in your research. For example, Water's guardians are Undines and their season is Autumn. Repeat with each of the four elements.

Element:

Image of element:

Direction:

Guardian:

Color:

Gems:

Season:

Time of Day:

Physical:

Abilities:

Herbs:

Notes:

Invoking Pentagram:

Banishing Pentagram:

GLOSSARY

A

Affirmations: A belief that repetitive, positive, assertive thoughts will influence people and reality.

Air: One of the four elements, considered the building blocks of everything. In many magical traditions, air corresponds with east, the color yellow, the mind, intelligence, and imagination.

Altar: A special, flat surface set aside exclusively for magical workings or religious/spiritual acknowledgment.

Amulet: A magically charged, protective, object which deflects specific, usually negative energies.

Astral plane: A place generally conceptualized as an invisible parallel world that remains unseen from our own solid world of form.

Astral projection: The process of separating your astral, or nonmaterial, body from your physical one to accomplish travel in the astral plane.

Astrology: The study of and belief in the effects the movements and placements of planets and other heavenly bodies have on the lives and behavior of human beings.

Athame: The Witch's knife. Although generally pronounced *a-tha-may*, the term is of obscure origin, has many variant spellings, and an even greater variety of pronunciations (*ah-THAM-ee* to rhyme with "whammy"; *ATH-ah-may* or *ah-THAW-may*).

Attunement: An activity which brings the minds, emotions, and psyches of a group into harmony prior to ritual: chanting, singing, guided meditation, and breathing exercises are common ways to attune.

Aura: The energy field of the human body, and especially that radiant portion visible to the third-eye or psychic vision. The aura can reveal information about an individual's health and emotional state.

B

Banishing: the magical act of driving away evil or negativity, sometimes associated with the removal of spirits.

Bell: Often used as a ritual tool, bells can be used to invoke directional energies or cleanse a space. Associated with the element of air.

Besom: A Witch's broom, used for sweeping away energies among other things.

Bolline: A white-handled knife, usually with a silver, sickle-shaped blade, used in magic for carving, cutting materials, or harvesting herbs.

Book of Shadows: A Witch's book of rituals, spells, dreams, herbal recipes, magical lore, and so forth.

British Traditional Witchcraft: Traditions tracing descent from a hereditary British source. Includes the Gardnerian Traditions and their offshoots but also several others derived from British sources such as Sybil Leek's Horsa Coven in the New Forest, Plant Bran, and the Clan of Tubal Cain of "Robert Cochrane." The term "British Traditional Wicca" is sometimes used, more commonly in the United States than elsewhere.

C

Cakes and ale: The sharing of a beverage and food offered to each participant in a ritual or eaten by participants at the end of the ritual as part of the grounding process.

Call: To invoke divine and elemental forces.

Cardinal point: North, east, south, and west. Often marked in the circle with candles or other items.

Casting the Circle: The psychic creation of a sphere of energy around the area where a ritual is to be performed, both to concentrate and focus the power raised, and to keep out unwanted influences or distractions. The space enclosed exists outside of ordinary space and time.

Cauldron: Representing the womb of the Goddess, it may be three- or four-legged. Most modern practitioners use it as a symbol, for cooking during ritual, to burn things in as part of a spell, or for scrying.

Censer: A heat-proof container in which incense is burned. It is associated with the element of air.

Centering: The process of moving one's consciousness to one's spiritual center, leading to a feeling of great peace, calmness, strength, clarity, and stability.

Ceremonial magic: A highly codified magical tradition based on Kabbala, the Jewish-Gnostic mystical teachings.

Chalice: A ritual tool representing the female principle of creation or the element of water.

Channeling: A practice in which you allow a discarnate entity to "borrow" your body to communicate.

Chant: This can be a rhyme intoned rhythmically to raise power. Such rhymes can be simple and repetitive, making them easier to remember.

Charging: Infusing an object with personal power as an act of magic.

Charm: An amulet or talisman that has been charged and instilled with energy for a specific task.

Circle: Sacred space wherein all magic is to be worked and all ritual contained. Also a term used to describe a gathering of Witches or Pagans. (It can get a little confusing: "Our circle is having a circle where we will circle in a circle.")

Cleansing: The act of removing negative energies from an object or space.

Collective unconsciousness: Term used to describe the sentient connection of all living things, past and present; also called the Akashic Records.

Cone of power: Psychic energy raised and focused during ritual to achieve a defined purpose.

Conscious mind: The analytical, materially based, rational half of our consciousness. This part of our mind is at work while we balance our checkbooks, theorize, communicate, and perform other acts related to the physical world.

Consecrate: To declare or set apart as sacred; to produce the ritual transformation of an item into sacred.

Correspondences: A system of symbolic equivalencies used in magic. *See also* Magical Correspondences.

Coven: One name for a group of Witches that work together in an organized fashion for positive magical endeavors or to perform religious ceremonies.

Craft: Short for "the Craft of the Wise." Generally associated with the practical aspects of the religion.

Cross-quarter days: Refers to sabbats falling on the solstices or equinoxes. *See also* Sabbat.

D

Days of power: Days triggered by astrological occurrences, moon cycles or special events—your birthday, the start of your menstrual cycle, your dedication/initiation anniversary, etc. *See also* Sabbat.

Dedication: A solemn promise or vow made in ritual, usually used to formally dedicate oneself to a spiritual path. Anyone may dedicate themselves to Deity, or to a spiritual path.

Degrees: Levels of initiation representing spiritual or magical development as well as skill, knowledge, and experience within a specific group or tradition.

Deosil: Clockwise, the direction in which the shadow on a sundial moves as the sun appears to move across the sky. Opposite of widdershins, deosil is symbolic of life, positive magic, and positive energies.

Divination: The magical art of discovering the unknown by interpreting random patterns or symbols through the use of tools such as clouds, tarot cards, flames, and smoke. Divination contacts the psychic mind by dowsing the conscious mind through ritual and observation or of manipulation of tools.

Divine power: The unmanifested, pure energy that exists in Deity; the life force, the ultimate source of all things.

Drawing down the moon: A ritual performed during the full moon by Witches to empower themselves and unite their essence with a particular deity, usually the Goddess.

Drawing down the sun: A lesser known companion ritual to drawing down the moon in which the essence of the God is drawn into the body of a Witch.

Duality: The opposite of polarity. When used as a religious term, it separates two opposites such as good and evil and places those characteristics into two completely separate god-forms.

E

Earth: In many magical traditions, this element corresponds to the direction of north; the colors black, brown, and forest green; foundation, stability, the human body, all solid material things, and prosperity.

Earth magic or power: The energy that exists in stones, herbs, flames, wind, and other natural objects.

Earthing: Sending excess energy into the earth. Done in ritual after power has been raised and sent to its goal. *See also* Grounding.

Eclectic: A mixture of beliefs borrowed from various traditions and theologies rather than a single tradition or set of beliefs.

Elder: One who is recognized as an experienced leader, teacher, and counselor.

Elementals: Archetypal spirit beings associated with one of the four elements. See also Quarters.

Elements: Earth, air, fire, water—the building blocks of the universe; everything that exists contains one or more of these energies.

Energy: The natural vibration or power that we tap into or raise, in our spells and rituals. Some think of this as something raised or generated, while others think it is always there for the trained person to tap into and direct.

Equinox: One of two events a year when the sun crosses the equator and day and night are of equal length, on or about March 21 and September 23.

Esbat: A ritual occurring on a lunar phase (dark, new, or full) and usually dedicated to the Goddess in her lunar aspect.

Evocation: To call something out from within.

F

Fire: In many traditions, the element corresponding to the south, the color red, energy, will, passion, determination, purpose, ambition, and spirituality.

First quarter: One half of the moon appears illuminated by direct sunlight while the illuminated part is increasing. In this phase, the moon is associated with the Maiden/Mother aspect of the Goddess.

Folklore: Traditional sayings, stories, cures, and wisdom of a particular locale, separate from their mythology.

Folk magic: The practice of projecting personal power, as well as the energies in natural objects, such as herbs and crystals, to bring about needed changes.

Full moon: The visible moon is fully illuminated by direct sunlight. Here the moon is associated with the Mother aspect of the Goddess.

G

Gaea/Gaia: The Earth, seen as a living though supernatural entity.

God: Masculine aspect of Deity. *See also* Lord.

Goddess: Feminine aspect of Deity. *See also* Lady.

Grimoire: A magical workbook with information on rituals, magical properties of natural objects, and preparation of ritual equipment. Many include a catalog of spirits. One of the most famous is *The Key of Solomon.*

Grounding: The process of connecting and aligning one's physical energy to the energy of the earth.

Guardians: The beings that protect the four quadrants or elements, of the Circle. *See also* Quarters.

H

Hand, projective: The right hand, which emits energies. NOTE: Switch if left-handed!

Hand, receptive: The left hand, which receives energies. NOTE: Switch if left-handed!

Healing: The goal of a great deal of magic, especially among healing-oriented spiritual traditions, is healing. Some alternative forms of healing include chakra/energy work, visualization, herbalism, spirit journeys, crystal healing, among many others.

Herbalism: Art of using herbs both magically and medicinally to facilitate human needs.

Hex: See Curse.

High Priest: Traditionally, the primary male leader in a coven, usually a 3rd degree initiate who was either chosen by the High Priestess or elected by members.

High Priestess: Traditionally, the primary female leader in a coven, usually a Third Degree initiate.

Higher self: That part of us which connects our corporeal minds to the collective unconscious and with the divine knowledge of the universe.

Hiving off: The process in which a coven splits off part of itself to form a new separate entity, generally in the same tradition. Although sometimes done to keep the coven a manageable size, it may also occur when irreconcilable philosophical or political differences arise.

Horned God: One of the most prevalent gods in Paganism.

I

Immanence: The belief that Deity exists in all things, including people, and cannot be separated from them.

Incense: Ritual burning of herbs, oils, or other aromatic items to scent the air during acts of magic and ritual, and to better help the Witch attune to the goal of the working.

Initiation: A ritual during which an individual is introduced or admitted into a magical group. Different from dedication. Initiation is specific to a group, although there are some rare examples of direct initiation by Deity. That said, only covens use degrees.

Intuition: A term describing psychic information that unexpectedly reaches the conscious mind.

Invocation: To bring something in from without. An appeal or petition to a higher power or powers, such as Deity, usually in the form of prayer. Invocation is a method of establishing conscious ties with aspects of Deity that dwell within.

K

Karma: Originally a Hindu belief that a person's thoughts and deeds can influence their personal future, usually across several lifetimes. Now widely accepted in Western popular culture and New Age spiritualities.

L

Lady: The Goddess; any of the names of her aspects. She is a triple goddess—Maiden, Mother, and Crone. She is all encompassing, containing especially all creative and procreative properties, all aspects of nurturing and healing, all forms of birth and rebirth, all growth and plenty. All women partake of her nature and are part of her. All things are her children.

Last quarter: Half of the moon appears illuminated by direct sunlight as the illuminated part is decreasing. Here the moon is seen as the Crone aspect of the Goddess.

Law of Return: Whatever energy is sent out returns to the sender multiplied. Some traditions say it is multiplied by three and therefore call this principle the "Threefold Law."

Laws of Witchcraft: A list of rules for Witches focusing on individual conduct and coven operations. They are sometimes called ordains; several versions exist. Generally, each coven has a set of laws, sometimes divided into spiritual, physical or mundane, and magical categories.

Libation: Ritually-given portion of food or drink to a deity, nature spirit, or ghost.

Lord: The God; any of the names of his aspects. He is the Horned God of the Hunt, the Lord of Death and Resurrection, the Laughing Lord. He is consort of the Lady, who dies and is reborn each year. He is sensuality, strength, music, and lust. All men partake of his nature and are part of him. He is the sun, the sky, and the wind.

Lunar cycle: Spanning roughly 29 days during which the visible phase of the moon waxes from dark to full and wanes to dark again. Much magic is geared to the energies present in certain phases of this cycle.

M

Macrocosm: The world around us.

Magic: Using knowledge and focused will to direct energy and manifest a change in physical reality.

Magic circle: A sphere constructed of personal power in which rituals are performed. In it, the Witch is protected from outside forces. The sphere extends both above and below the surface of the ground.

Magic, sympathetic: The concept of like attracts like, the most common manner in which spells are worked.

Magical correspondences: Items, objects, days, colors, moon phases, oils, angels, and herbs used in a ritual or magical working that match the intent or purpose of the celebration or ceremony.

Magical system: The basic set of guidelines relating to the worship of specific gods and goddesses or cultural traditions. Also called a tradition.

Maiden: Youngest aspect of the Triple Goddess. Represented by the waxing moon and the colors white and blue; her sabbats are Imbolc and Ostara.

Male mysteries: A field of Pagan study that aims to reclaim the power and mystery of the old gods for today's Pagan males.

Meditation: Reflection, contemplation—turning inward toward the self, or outward toward Deity or nature. A quiet time in which the practitioner may either dwell upon particular thoughts or symbols or allow them to come unbidden.

Microcosm: The world in us.

Mighty Ones: Beings, deities, unseen presences usually invoked during rituals and/or ceremonies. Sometimes linked to the elements. *See also* Old Ones.

Mind, conscious: The controlled, intellectual part of mind that does everyday work; the rational part that thinks.

Mind, psychic: The subconscious or unconscious mind in which we receive psychic impulses. The psychic mind is at work when we sleep, dream, and meditate.

Monotheism: Belief in one supreme deity who has no other forms or displays no other aspects.

Mother: The aspect of the Goddess representing motherhood, mid-life, and fertility. She is represented by the full moon, the egg, and the colors red and green; her sabbats are Midsummer and Lammas.

N

Natural fiber: In reference to textiles, cotton, linen (from flax), silk, and wool.

Neopagan: A member of newly formed religions now forming worldwide. All Witches are Pagan, but not all Pagans are Witches.

Nontheistic Pagan: A Pagan who works energy and otherwise behaves as a Witch but does not ascribe personification, particular worship, or godhood to the energy they raise.

O

Occult: From Latin *occulere*, meaning "hidden," universally applied to a wide range of metaphysical topics that lay outside the accepted realm of mainstream theologies; To conceal and hide away knowledge from the uninitiated.

Old Ones: A term used to encompass all aspects of the God and Goddess. Alternative of Mighty Ones.

Old Religion: Another Craft term, which fits the song, "Give me that Old Time Religion" much better than the Christian use of it.

Ordains: The traditional laws of the Craft.

P

Pagan: From the Latin *paganus*, "country dweller." One who practices a religion not part of the Abrahamic or Hindu, Muslim, Buddhist mainstream. All Witches are Pagan, not all Pagans are Witches.

Pantheon: A collection or group of gods and goddesses in a particular religious or mythical structure.

Pantheism: Belief in many deities; Paganism is pantheistic.

Pentacle: A circle surrounding a five-pointed, upright star (pentagram). Often worn as a symbol of a Witch's beliefs, the circle represents: unity or the World.

Pentagram: The basic interlaced five-pointed star, visualized with one point up. It represents the elements earth, air, fire, water, and spirit, and is a symbol of power and protection.

Pendulum: A divinatory tool consisting of a device hanging from a string; its movement is the deciphered and interpreted. This tool contacts the psychic mind.

Plane, mental: The thought process, conscious and unconscious.

Plane, physical: The physical body and its workings, through coordination with mental plane.

Plane, spiritual: A person's perception of life's existence, consisting of belief or lack of belief in the Divine.

Polarity: The concept of equal but opposite energies or powers. For example: Goddess/God, night/day, moon/sun, birth/death, dark/light, psychic mind/conscious mind.

Polytheism: Belief in the existence of many unrelated deities each with their own dominion and interests who have no spiritual or familial relationships to one another.

Power, personal: The energies which sustain the body and are used in magic.

Priest: A male dedicated to both the service of his chosen deity and humankind.

Priestess: A female dedicated to both the service of her chosen deity and humankind.

Priestex: A person dedicated to both the service of their chosen deity and humankind. This is a gender-neutral term that can be used when a person's gender is undefined, unknown, or irrelevant.

Psychic Mind: The subconscious, or unconscious mind, in which we receive psychic impressions. It is at work when we sleep, dream, and meditate. It is our direct link with the Divine, and with the larger, nonphysical world around us.

Psychic Trance: When a person enters the altered state of consciousness in which he or she is no longer using the normal beta waves associated with ordinary consciousness, but instead the theta and delta waves associated with sleep. A Witch enters this state to do acts of magic.

Psychism: The act of being consciously psychic, in which the psychic mind and conscious mind are linked and working in harmony. Also known as psychic awareness. Psychokinesis: the act of mind over matter, or mind controlling matter by mind alone.

Q

Quarters: Either the cardinal directions, corresponding to the elements and protected by the Guardians, or the sabbats that fall on equinoxes or solstices.

R

Rede: "An it harm none, do what thou wilt."

Reincarnation: The process of repeated incarnations in human form to allow evolution of the sexless, ageless soul. The belief that souls do not end at death but wait for a time and then are reborn to live and learn on this earth again.

Ritual: A specific form of movement, a manipulation of objects or inner processes designed to produce desired effects. In religion, ritual is geared toward union with the Divine. In magical works it produces a specific state of consciousness that allows the Witch to move energy toward needed goals.

Ritual consciousness: A specific alternate state of awareness necessary to the successful practice of magic.

Ritual tools: A general name for magical tools. They vary by tradition and usually represent one of the elements.

Runes: Divination tools, remnant of ancient Teutonic alphabets. A set of symbols used both in divination and magical work.

S

Sabbat: One of eight holidays; a time for feasting, partying, and general merrymaking. The word *sabbat* has various derivations, but I prefer the argument that it comes from the French *s'ebattre*, "to frolic." *See also* Wheel of the Year.

Scourge: Small device made from leather or hemp resembling a whip, used in flagellation rites in some traditions.

Scrying: A method of divination involving gazing at or into an object such as a quartz crystal sphere, a pool of water, reflection, or candle flame while stilling the conscious mind in order to contact the psychic mind. Scrying allows the scryer to become aware of events prior to their actual occurrence, as well as to perceive past or present events through other than the five senses.

Secular: Material and worldly as opposed to spiritual; thus, anything not religious.

Shrine: A sacred place that holds a collection of objects representing a deity.

Sky clad: A term meaning nude, usually referring to state of undress while doing rituals.

Solstice: Occurring twice a year midway between the two equinoxes, producing a day with the shortest light and longest dark hours in December and a day of longest light and shortest dark hours in June. The solstice occurs on or near the 21st of the months.

Spell: A magical ritual sometimes non-religious in nature, often accompanied by spoken words. It is the extension of mental and emotional energy to accomplish a specific goal. A spell can be written, spoken, drawn, and so on.

Spiral: A symbol that signifies an inward journey. It represents the emergence into consciousness of what was previously hidden. It also suggests the round of seasons, where life unfolds, fades, and unfolds again in a repeating cycle.

Spiral, double: A symbol of the Witch's descent into the Underworld and subsequent rebirth from death into life.

Spirit: The overall energy that runs the universe in a harmonious way; the fifth element.

T

Taboo: Forbidden object or exercise.

Talisman: An object charged with personal power to attract a specific force or energy to its bearer.

Tarot: The name given to a special deck of cards used as a tool for divinatory purpose. Traditionally numbering seventy-eight cards, of which twenty-one make up the major arcana. The minor arcana are divided into four suits—cups, wands, pentacles, and swords.

Tasseography: A form of divination in which tea leaves are read.

Telepathy: The act of thought transference.

Threefold Law: See Law of Return.

Tools: Instruments, empowered with magic; used by Witches. Includes runes, tarot, candles, crystals, wands, censers, and so on. Tools require physical cleansing and consecration, prior to use for ceremonial purposes.

Traditions: Branches of Witchcraft followed by specific covens. Characterized by specific beliefs and practices that may never be shared with outsiders.

Trance: An altered state of consciousness.

Triple Goddess: One goddess who has three aspects: Maiden, Mother, Crone.

V

Visualization: The process of forming mental images. Magical visualization consists of forming images of desired goals during ritual and may be used to direct personal power and natural energies for various purposes, including charging and forming of the magic circle.

W

Wand: Ritual tool usually representing fire.

Warlock: This word is not usually used for a male Witch. Its meaning comes from the Old English (one source: Scottish) *waerloga*, meaning an untrustworthy man, an oath breaker, or sometimes a eunuch.

Water: In most magical traditions, this element corresponds with west, the color blue, the psychic mind, intuition, and emotion.

Waxing crescent: In this phase, the visible moon is partly but less than one-half illuminated by direct sunlight while the illuminated part is increasing. The Moon here is Maiden.

Waxing gibbous: The Moon is more than one-half but not fully illuminated by direct sunlight while the illuminated part is increasing. Three days before the full moon.

Waxing moon: The phase of the moon in which the face of the moon is getting larger. The time between a new moon and a full moon.

Wheel of the Year: The full cycle of the eight sabbats in the Witches' calendar, occurring at the equinoxes, solstices, and on the days marking the midpoints between. A short list of the names used by my tradition:

Name(s)	Dates
Yule	Winter Solstice
Imbolc	February 2
Ostara	Spring Equinox
Beltane	April 30
Litha	Summer Solstice
Lammas	August 2
Autumn Equinox	Autumn Equinox
Samhain	October 31

Wicca: A modern Pagan religion with spiritual roots in the earliest expressions of reverence for nature. Some major identifying motifs are: reverence for a dual-gendered deity (Goddess and God); belief in reincarnation; ritual observance of astronomical and agricultural phenomena; and a commonality of ritual format. Often used instead of "Witchcraft;" similarly, "Witch" and "Wiccan" are often used interchangeably.

Widdershins: Counter-clockwise motion, opposite of deosil. Usually used for inward-looking magical purposes or for dispersing negative energies or conditions such as disease.

Witch: A practitioner of the "Craft of the Wise," this term applies equally to everyone, regardless of gender. Used by some Wiccans to describe themselves.

Witchcraft: The craft of the Witch—magic, especially magic using personal power in conjunction with the energies in stones, herbs, colors, and other natural objects.

Witches' Pyramid: A creed and a structure of learning that Witches follow: To Know, To Dare, To Will, and To Be Silent.

BIBLIOGRAPHY

Adler, Margot. *Drawing Down the Moon: Witches, Druids, Goddess-Worshippers, and Other Pagans in America.* New York: Viking Press, 1979.

Allen, LaSara Firefox. *Jailbreaking the Goddess: A Radical Revisioning of Feminist Spirituality.* Woodbury, MN: Llewellyn Publications, 2016.

Beyerl, Paul. *Master Book of Herbalism.* Custer, WA: Phoenix Publishing, 1984.

Blake, Deborah. *Witchcraft on a Shoestring: Practicing the Craft Without Breaking Your Budget.* Woodbury, MN: Llewellyn Publications, 2010.

Blum, Ralph. *The Book of Runes.* London: Michael Joseph Ltd, 1984.

Bonewits, Isaac. *Real Magic: An Introductory Treatise on the Basic Principles of Yellow Magic.* Boston: Red Wheel/Weiser, 1989.

Bonewits, Isaac, and Phaedra Bonewits. *Real Energy: Systems, Spirits, and Substances to Heal, Change, and Grow.* Wayne, NJ: New Page Books, 2007.

Campbell, Joseph. *The Hero's Journey: Joseph Campbell on His Life and Work, 3rd Edition.* Novato, CA: New World Library, 2003.

Campbell, Joseph, and Bill Moyers. *The Power of Myth.* New York: Anchor Books, 1991.

Conway, D. J. *Maiden, Mother, Crone: The Myth & Reality of the Triple Goddess*. St. Paul, MN: Llewellyn Publications, 1997.

Cuhulain, Kerr. *Wiccan Warrior: Walking a Spiritual Path in a Sometimes Hostile World*. St. Paul, MN: Llewellyn Publications, 2000.

Cunningham, Scott. *Cunningham's Book of Shadows: The Path of An American Traditionalist*. Woodbury, MN: Llewellyn Publications, 2009.

———. *The Complete Book of Incense, Oils & Brews*. St. Paul, MN: Llewellyn Publications, 1986.

———. *Earth, Air, Fire & Water: More Techniques of Natural Magic*. St. Paul, MN: Llewellyn Publications, 1991.

———. *Earth Power: Techniques of Natural Magic*. St. Paul, MN: Llewellyn Publications, 1991.

Decoz, Hans. *Numerology: A Complete Guide to Understanding and Using Your Numbers of Destiny*. New York: Penguin-Putnam, 2001.

Dominguez Jr., Ivo. *Casting Sacred Space: The Core of All Magical Work*. Boston: Weiser, 2012.

Farrar, Janet, and Gavin Bone. *Progressive Witchcraft: Spirituality, Mysteries, and Training in Modern Wicca*. Boston: Red Wheel.Weiser, 2003.

Farrar, Stewart, and Janet Farrar. *A Witches' Bible: The Complete Witches' Handbook*. Blaine, WA: Phoenix Publishing, 1996.

Fitch, Ed. *Magical Rites from the Crystal Well*. St. Paul, MN: Llewellyn Publication, 1984.

Foley, Michael P. *Why Do Catholics Eat Fish on Friday?: The Catholic Origin to Just About Everything*. London: Palgrave Macmillan, 2005.

Fortune, Dion. *Aspects of Occultism*, rev. edition. Boston: Weiser, 2000. First published 1962 by Aquarian Press (Northamptonshire, UK).

———. *The Sea Priestess*. Boston: Weiser, 2003. First published 1935 by The Inner Light Publishing Co. (London).

Gardner, Gerald, *The Meaning of Witchcraft*. Boston: Weiser, 2004. First published 1959 by Aquarian Press (London).

———. *Witchcraft Today*. Secaucus, NJ: Citadel Press, 1974. First published 1954 by Rider & Co. (London).

Guiley, Rosemary Ellen. *The Encyclopedia of Witches, Witchcraft and Wicca, 3rd Edition*. New York: Checkmark Books, 2008.

Harner, Michael. *The Way of the Shaman*. New York: Bantam Books, 1982.

Hiroven, Joonas. "Animals and Demons: Faunal Appearances, Metaphors, and Similes in Lamastu Incantations." Mattila, Raija, et. al. eds. *Animals and their Relation to Gods, Humans and Things in the Ancient World*. Frankfurt, Germany: VS Verlag für Sozialwissenschaften, 2019.

Hutton, Ronald. *The Stations of the Sun: A History of the Ritual Year in Britain*. Oxford, UK: Oxford University Press, 1996.

———. *Triumph of the Moon: A History of Modern Pagan Witchcraft*. Oxford, UK: Oxford University Press, 2001.

Jacobi, Jolande. *The Psychology of C.G. Jung*. New Haven: Yale University Press. 1973.

Jung, C.G. *The Collected Works of C.G. Jung*. Princeton: Princeton University Press. 1953.

K, Amber. *RitualCraft: Creating Rites for Transformation and Celebration*. St. Paul: Llewellyn Publications, 2006.

Kraig, Donald Michael. *Modern Magic: Twelve Lessons in the High Magical Arts*. Woodbury, MN: Llewellyn Publications, 2010.

Kraemer, Christine Hoff, and Yvonne Aburrow, eds. *Pagan Consent Culture: Building Communities of Empathy and Autonomy*. Hubbardston, MA: Asphodel Press, 2016.

L, Frater. "Stregha." *Journal of the Western Mystery Tradition* 1, no. 6 (2004). http://jwmt.org/v1n6/stregha.html.

Lamond, Frederic. *Fifty Years of Wicca*. Glastonbury, UK: Green Magic, 2005.

Lawson, David. *Principles of Self-Healing*. New York: Thorsons Publishing, 1996.

Leitch, Aaron. "Modern Grimoire Magic: Folk Magic and The Solomonic Path." *Journal of the Western Mystery Tradition* 1, no. 10, (2006). http://www.jwmt.org/v1n10/modern.html.

———. *Secrets of the Magickal Grimoires: The Classical Texts of Magic Deciphered*. St. Paul, MN: Llewellyn Publications, 2005.

Leitch, Aaron. *The Angelical Language, Volume II: An Encyclopedic Lexicon of the Tongue of Angels*. Woodbury, MN: Llewellyn Publications, 2010.

Lévi, Éliphas. *Transcendental Magic: Its Doctrine and Ritual*. London: William Rider & Son, 1923.

Linn, Denise. *Altars: Bringing Sacred Shrines into Your Everyday Life*. New York: Ballantine Publishing, 1999.

Lipp, Deborah. *The Elements of Ritual Air, Fire, Water & Earth in the Wiccan Circle*. St. Paul, MN: Llewellyn Publications, 2003.

Lupa. *Fang and Fur, Blood and Bone, revised edition*. Self-published, 2020.

Lust, John B. *The Herb Book: The Most Complete Catalog of Herbs Ever Published*. New York: Bantam Books, 1980.

Mankey, Jason. *The Witch's Book of Shadows*. Woodbury, MN: Llewellyn Publications, 2009.

Mankey, Jason, and Laura Tempest Zakroff. *The Witch's Altar: The Craft, Lore & Magic of Sacred Space*. Woodbury, MN: Llewellyn Publications, 2018.

Mariechild, Diane. *Mother Wit: A Feminist Guide to Psychic Development*. Berkeley, CA: Crossing Press, 1981.

McFarland, Phoenix. *The New Book of Magical Names*. St. Paul, MN: Llewellyn Publications, 2003.

McKim, Robert. *Experiences in Visual Thinking, second ed.* Boston: Cengage Learning, 1980.

McSherry, Lisa. *The Virtual Pagan: Exploring Wicca and Paganism through the Internet*. York Beach, ME: Red Wheel/Weiser, 2002.

———. *Magical Connections: Creating a Lasting and Healthy Spiritual Group*. Secaucus, NJ: New Page Books, 2007.

Melton, Gordon B., and Martin Baumann, eds. *Religions of the World: A Comprehensive Encyclopedia of Beliefs and Practices*. Santa Barbara, CA: ABC-CLIO, 2010.

Millman, Dan. *Way of the Peaceful Warrior: A Basically True Story*. New York: Houghton Mifflin, 1980.

Moore, Robert, and Gillette, Douglas. *The Warrior Within: Accessing the Knight in the Male Psyche*. New York: HarperCollins, 1992.

Nichols, Mike. *The Witches' Sabbat*. Portland, OR: Acorn Guild Press, 2005.

Nichols, Sallie. *Jung and Tarot: An Archetypal Journey*. Boston: Weiser Books, 1980.

Nielsen, Morten Ebbe Juul. "Safe, Sane, and Consensual—Consent and the Ethics of BDSM." *The International Journal of Applied Philosophy* 24, no. 2 (2010).

NIIR Board of Consultants and Engineers, *Modern Technology of Printing & Writing Inks (with Formulae & Processes) 2nd revised edition*. Delhi, India: Asia Pacific Business Press, 2016.

Rich, Vivian. *Cursing the Basil and Other Folklore of the Garden*. Victoria, BC: Touchwood Editions, 2010.

Rochberg, Francesca. *Babylonian Horoscopes*. Philadelphia: American Philosophical Society, 1998.

Roth, Gabrielle. *Maps to Ecstasy: The Healing Power of Movement*. Novato, CA: New World Library. 1998.

———. *Sweat Your Prayers: The Five Rhythms of the Soul—Movement as Spiritual Practice*. New York: TarcherPerigee, 1998.

Salomonsen, Jone. *Enchanted Feminism: The Reclaiming Witches of San Francisco*. London: Routledge, 2002.

Sharp, Damian. *Simple Numerology*. Auckland, New Zealand: Castle, 2002.

Starhawk. *The Spiral Dance: A Rebirth of the Ancient Religion of the Great Goddess*. San Francisco: Harper San Francisco, 1980.

———. *Truth or Dare: Encounters with Power, Authority, and Mystery*. San Francisco: Harper San Francisco, 1989.

Strimska, Michael. *Modern Paganism in World Cultures: Comparative Perspectives*. Santa Barbara, CA: ABC-CLIO, 2005.

Tetlow, Elisabeth Meier. *Women, Crime and Punishment in Ancient Law and Society: Volume 1: The Ancient Near East*. New York: Continuum, 2004.

Thorsson, Edred. *Runelore: The Magic, History, and Hidden Codes of the Runes*. Boston: Weiser Books, 1987.

UCLA. "UCLA Mindful Awareness Research Center (MARC)." Accessed October 25, 2020. https://uclahealth.org/marc.

Valiente, Doreen. *The Rebirth of Witchcraft*. London: Robert Hale, 1989.

———. *An ABC of Witchcraft Past and Present*. New York: St. Martin's Press, 1973.

Valiente, Doreen, and Evan Jones. *Witchcraft: A Tradition Renewed*. Blaine, WA: Phoenix Publishing, 1990.

Weinstein, Marion. *Positive Magic: Occult Self-help*. Blaine, WA: Phoenix Publishing, 1978.

Wilby, Emma. *Cunning Folk and Familiar Spirits: Shamanistic Visionary Traditions in Early Modern British Witchcraft and Magic*. Cambridge, UK: Academic Press, 2005.

Wood, Robin. *When, Why, If…: An Ethics Workbook*. Dearborn, MI: Livingtree Books, 1996.

Various authors. "Internet Book of Shadows: Basic Principles of the Craft." Sacred Texts website. Accessed April 17, 2020. https://sacred-texts.com/bos/bos080.htm.

———. "The Finer Points of Ritual: A Comparative Approach to Liturgical History, Theology and Design." Sacred Texts website. Accessed May 11, 2020. https://www.sacred-texts.com/bos/bos632.htm.

———. Poe, Michael. "Ancient Egyptian Metaphysics." Accessed October 20, 2020. https://sacred-texts.com/bos/bos446.htm.

———. Rankine, David. "What Is Magic?" Accessed June 22, 2020. https://sacred-texts.com/bos/msg0001.htm.

———. Carmicheal, Alexander. *Carmina Gadelica, Volume 1*, 1900. Accessed May 6, 2020. https://sacred-texts.com/neu/celt/cg1/cg1074.htm.

———. "Grimoires." Accessed December 17, 2019. https://sacred-texts.com/grim.

———. Leland, Charles Godfrey. "Aradia." Accessed December 17, 2019. https://sacred-texts.com/pag/aradia.

Wikipedia.com. "Astrology." Accessed 2.2.20, https://en.wikipedia.org/wiki/Astrology.

———."Babylonia Astrology." Accessed 2.2.20. https://en.wikipedia.org/ wiki/Babylonian_astrology.

———."Enochian." Accessed 7.1.20, https://en.wikipedia.org/wiki/ Enochian.

———."Orientation of churches." Accessed 3.4.2020. https://en.wikipedia. org/wiki/Orientation_of_churches.

INDEX

TO WRITE TO THE AUTHOR

If you wish to contact the author or would like more information about this book, please write to the author in care of Llewellyn Worldwide Ltd. and we will forward your request. Both the author and publisher appreciate hearing from you and learning of your enjoyment of this book and how it has helped you. Llewellyn Worldwide Ltd. cannot guarantee that every letter written to the author can be answered, but all will be forwarded. Please write to:

Lisa McSherry
℅ Llewellyn Worldwide
2143 Wooddale Drive
Woodbury, MN 55125-2989

Please enclose a self-addressed stamped envelope for reply,
or $1.00 to cover costs. If outside the U.S.A., enclose
an international postal reply coupon.

Many of Llewellyn's authors have websites with additional
information and resources. For more information,
please visit our website at http://www.llewellyn.com